Workplace Violence Prevention Handbook for Health Care

Authors

Kimberly A. Urbanek

&

Kyle J. Graham

Contributors

Dr. Lindsey Harrington

Ravi Hookoom

Erica Howard

Katarina Kemper

Laura Larkin

Deb Somers-Larney

Published by Crisis Prevention Institute (CPI)

Milwaukee, Wisconsin

CRISIS PREVENTION INSTITUTE®

Published by
Crisis Prevention Institute
Milwaukee, Wisconsin

https://www.crisisprevention.com

CRISIS PREVENTION
INSTITUTE

Disclaimer
This handbook represents the experiences, perspectives, and
recommendations of the authors and contributors and should not
be used as a substitute for legal advice from competent attorneys
that are familiar with your current company policies and regulatory
guidelines that apply to your health care organization.

Interior design and book production by S4Carlisle Publishing Services,
Chennai, India

Cover design by Crisis Prevention Institute

Identifiers: ISBN 979-8-9864693-0-0 (print)/
ISBN 979-8-9864693-1-7 (ebook)

Published simultaneously in softcover and ebook formats in the United
States of America by Crisis Prevention Institute.

Contents

CPI

Foreword

CPI

Brine Hamilton

Workplace violence is arguably one of, if not the most impactful challenges in the healthcare environment. Workplace violence is expensive and can be expressed in many different ways including but not limited to verbal interactions, threats, intimidation, and of course physical violence. Since the start of the COVID-19 pandemic, the challenges related to workplace violence in healthcare have increased significantly. In Chapter 1, the authors bring this to the forefront, noting that a four-hospital organization documented that calls for public safety intervention to protect staff members more than doubled from 2019 to 2020. Unfortunately, this trend was not limited to a single organization.

Across North America, workplace violence figures demonstrate a widespread increase in the occurrence of violent events in healthcare facilities. The impact of workplace violence extends beyond the acts themselves. Those directly involved in the events, other staff members, patients, visitors, and, in more severe cases, the loved ones of all of those involved can be negatively impacted by workplace violence. Understanding that we have limited control over the behaviors of others, our ability to affect change, implement preventative measures, and improve event response can all be very impactful. It is evident that a proactive approach to preventing workplace violence is necessary if we hope to see a change in the current dynamics. This handbook was created to help facilitate that change.

Every healthcare organization is different. Some may be unsure where to start in terms of building a workplace violence prevention program, or some may have an established program and are seeking ways to improve upon what already exists. Whether looking to start from scratch or to enhance an experienced program, this handbook will be a valued resource, regardless of the maturity of the workplace violence prevention program. The 10 chapters in this handbook were created to support the organization and make ongoing improvements to the workplace violence prevention program by providing principles and information that will help establish a solid foundation, regardless of your role in your organization, or the type of healthcare facility you work in.

Are you new to healthcare or newly overseeing workplace violence prevention? Chapter 1 will help you gain an understanding of the challenges involved, while Chapter 2 will establish the components of a successful workplace violence prevention program or help make the necessary revisions to one that already exists. Chapters 3 and 4 focus on two elements that in my professional opinion do not get the attention warranted, which are follow-up and data collection. These topics are both critical components of an effective workplace violence prevention program. Chapters 5 and 6 will help to ensure you are engaging the most suitable stakeholders to support the workplace violence prevention team, while establishing and managing the appropriate training. Chapters 7 and 8 provide the foundation for building a culture of violence prevention built on communication and collaboration, while Chapters 9 and 10 examine more specialized use cases and arm you with some best practices and resources. I have no doubt that no matter where your workplace violence prevention program is today, this handbook can help strengthen your program to the benefit of those who deliver and receive care in your facility.

Perhaps the most valuable feature of this handbook is the multidisciplinary team of contributing authors from both Canada and the United States. Some of the authors I've had the privilege of meeting and working with professionally include Kimberly Urbanek and Katarina Kemper, while I know of Deb Somers-Larney because of her presence in healthcare security, all three of whom are respected thought leaders in my industry. Clinical perspectives from Kyle Graham, Erica Howard, Dr. Lindsey Harrington, Laura Larkin, and the knowledge of safety professional Ravi Hookoom not only provide valuable insights with a multidisciplinary approach but also serve as a demonstration of how a multidisciplinary workforce should collaborate to enhance workplace violence prevention programs in healthcare.

As you read this book, you'll notice that each chapter begins with a list of learning objectives highlighting what you'll need to know or what you will learn from each chapter, and how it can be applied. Throughout the book you will find illustrations, tables, and examples that will benefit you as you are learning. As you conclude each chapter, you will find references and a glossary of terms, as well as a full glossary of terms with page references at the end of the book. No matter your role in healthcare, whether you are facing the patients daily, serving in an educational capacity providing staff training, part of a workplace violence committee, a C-Suite level executive, and everywhere in between, the knowledge gained from this book will enhance your performance.

In my experience, working in healthcare facilities, volunteering with leading industry associations including the International Association for Healthcare Security and Safety (IAHSS) and ASIS International, conducting podcast interviews with healthcare security leaders, and in my current roles in which I work with hundreds of healthcare leaders in the United States and Canada, I can attest that workplace violence prevention is top-of-mind on a daily basis. Adding this book to your library of resources and applying the learnings to your day-to-day operations are a positive step toward reducing the negative impacts of workplace violence prevention in your facility.

The authors, contributors, and publisher have made an important contribution to the field by bringing this project to fruition.

Preface

The Goal of the Handbook

Verbal abuse, name-calling, threats, and even physical violence have become the daily reality of working in the health care field. What were once occasional incidents are now familiar experiences among staff who have grown accustomed to having to navigate these rough waters. The prevalence of workplace violence (WPV) has been examined and documented but has yet to be stopped in the health care arena. There are seemingly endless consequences due to this growing epidemic that negatively impacts not just staff members, but patients and their families as well. Some of these impacts can be measured and are more obvious, like staff turnover, injury rates, cost of worker's compensation, and lost workdays. However, there are many other impacts that are harder to capture in any type of specific measurement. Compassion fatigue, burnout, low morale, frustration, fear, resentment, and hesitation are only some of the psychological consequences that WPV events can have on staff. Although most health care organizations already have existing policies or parameters in place to generally address or meet required standards, a large majority of leadership and staff have expressed that the plans and prevention protocols are not as effective as they could or should be. Understanding that leadership and staff alike all want a resolution to WPV, there are many difficulties that get in the way of bridging the gap in organizational prevention programs. That is where this handbook comes in.

This handbook was created to assist with managing the complex topic of WPV in health care. It is designed to serve as a reference manual to fill the gaps that commonly exist in health care organizations, by providing a reasonable and practical approach, based on expert knowledge and field experience. The intended goal for this handbook is for it to be used as a planning guide and resource to complement an organization's existing program or assist with the creation of a new program. This handbook will initially provide a general overview of WPV, but it goes beyond that, as it leads organizations to brainstorm specific initiatives that can be implemented in their own environment. Through transparency and best practices compiled from diverse health care experts and disciplines, an organization can use this handbook as a recipe for how to successfully steer their teams to a safer daily experience.

The Audience for the Handbook

This handbook was written specifically for anyone affiliated with the health care industry in North America. From Canada to the United States, the content of this handbook is intended to be flexible enough so that any health care professional or health care organization can benefit from it. Hospitals, clinics, long-term care facilities, outpatient departments, dental offices, or ambulatory surgery centers can all utilize this manual. The material presented here has value to all organizations as they can tailor the ideas presented here to address the needs of their own staff. In addition, this handbook was intended to be used by all job titles, from frontline staff to CEOs and board members. To truly have a state-of-the-art workplace violence prevention (WPVP) program, every person and every discipline within an organization needs to have the same core understanding of what a program consists of. Whether reading this as a leader at the organization, a trainer, a nurse, or even a financial planner, the curriculum covered in this handbook is meant to be universal. Chapters are designed to target individual topics in a comprehensive way so that a reader can select the areas that will be most beneficial to them.

How It All Began

Over the past several years, there has been a growing interest in WPVP in health care. Due to the growing number of incidents in health care, and the inability to move the needle on improvements, WPV has garnered the attention of many professional organizations and regulatory agencies as well. We (Kim and Kyle) both have a passion for WPVP and have championed the need for prevention strategies in the workplace for years. We have both participated in multiple trainings, studies, surveys, and focus groups over the years and have done quite a bit of research as well, all relating to WPVP. We have coached and consulted others on the topic as well. The idea for this handbook actually came out of research and focus groups conducted by the Crisis Prevention Institute (CPI) in 2020 regarding violence in the health care industry and best practices among WPVP committees. We were both participants in the CPI study and were left with unanswered questions after hearing what our peers had to say and the struggles that were discussed. There were common themes that surfaced, and we heard and felt a desire to continue to network with others regarding this topic. When the session ended, the conversation around WPVP just didn't feel complete.

Apparently, we weren't the only ones who thought that. Upon reviewing the data from the multiple focus groups, CPI also felt that there was much more to discuss on this topic as did the other participants. Though the intent of the focus groups was never about writing a book, the idea for this handbook came from those focus group findings. CPI conducted additional surveys and research, and it became apparent that there was a need to share best practices in relation to WPVP. We heard loud and clear that various areas across the health care industry gained value from the discussions and were curious about what other organizations were doing. There were clear gaps and deficits and a craving to know what was working and what wasn't working for others. We were all trying to navigate this endeavor, but it was clear that it's hard to find transparency about "how" people are making improvements within their program.

That's when CPI approached us to coauthor a handbook on WPV for the health care industry. As subject matter experts, CPI offered us the chance to write about what we know best. We selected the critical topics that needed to be addressed, based on our experience as well as research and data from surveys and focus groups. We selected additional contributors from the United States and Canada to ensure we included a variety of professionals with real-life experience that could offer expert input. Over the last 6 months, we compiled the best data out there to include in this handbook. We plan to update this handbook in the future, to keep it relevant and worthy of your time and effort. Going forward, we hope to collaborate with our readers and other experts to continue to add value in future versions. Until then, we present version one of this handbook.

The Format

This handbook consists of 10 chapters, with each chapter being able to stand alone, not requiring someone to read from cover to cover. The initial chapters start with the broad strokes of how to establish a WPV program while further chapters take a deeper dive into the specifics around initiatives and culture change.

Each chapter outlines performance objectives and provides some background knowledge as to the importance of the chapter. The content of each chapter expands on each of the objectives. Below is more information on the layout of this handbook.

- Chapter 1 serves as an introduction to WPVP in health care.
- Chapters 2 – 9 are organized around key topics that are important for you and your organization, based on our experience and research results.
- Chapter 10 is focused on providing additional references, resources, and templates to use to build from; this chapter will continue to evolve and will later incorporate feedback and best practices from readers.
- Each chapter has references to research data and studies.
- Each chapter has a working glossary with words that are in bold, indicating they can be found in the glossary.
- There is a comprehensive, indexed glossary with definitions and page references at the end of the handbook.

The Future of WPVP in Health Care Organizations

WPVP efforts will indeed be an important topic in the future of health care. However, collaboration is the key for us to evolve and improve the state of violence in the workplace. Collaboration will be needed to achieve transparency in our industry, and collaboration will be needed to ensure organizations can commit to a robust training program for staff. If we strive to prevent violence and not just react to it, then it's essential to have consistency across not only the individual organization, but across all health care systems and industries (health care, education, social work, mental health, etc.). We need to have a unified approach to first establish and then support a culture of violence pre-vention across all communities, states/provinces, and countries. We need transparency to standardize data collection, quality improvement initiatives, and subsequent metrics. We need to prioritize and finance ongoing training to prepare staff in relevant, meaningful ways. If we can all share our successes and failures, we will rapidly move toward a safer industry in the future. In an effort to work toward this goal, we will continue to bring updated ideas and best practices forward.

Acknowledgments

We have to begin by thanking CPI and its visionary leaders for the decision to act upon their research and gut instincts, to bring this handbook to life. Special thanks to Susan Driscoll, CPI's President, for her belief in the importance of this project and the need to raise the dialogue level around WPVP.

We want to acknowledge the contributors we worked with along the way. They brought their expertise and passion to this project, and we cannot thank them enough. Thank you to Deb, Lindsey, Laura, Ravi, Erica, and Kat who helped bring value to this book and were always receptive to our ideas, edits, and revisions. All of the contributors, and the two of us, owe special thanks to our many colleagues and industry peers that provided insight and information to us over the years. This was valuable as we worked to develop our chapters.

As mentioned, the idea for this handbook grew out of focus group conversations conducted by CPI. A debt of gratitude is owed to the participants that shared their perspectives and insights during these focus groups. Those conversations were helpful as we began to outline the necessary content for the handbook.

Much of our work on the handbook was guided by David Brake and Renee Covert of The Grandview Group, working on special assignment as our publisher and production manager. Thanks for putting up with all our questions and helping to guide us on this journey. A special thanks to Renee for all the behind-the-scenes support you provided and your diligent way of keeping us on track.

Special Acknowledgments from Kyle

I would like to give special thanks to my wife Stefani and our kids Graeson and Briar for their never-ending love and support, especially during this project. WPVP has been a passion for both Kim and I, for many years being a strong focus both educationally and professionally. The thought of collaborating on this handbook seemed like a great idea and we both embraced the challenge of finding contributors and bringing people together across the continent, all with the common goal of advancing WPVP through creating an easy-to-understand and accessible handbook. Kim thank you for sharing your passion and dedication for WPVP with me, and for being such a dedicated partner. Working alongside you over the past 6 months has been a pleasure and has taught me so much.

I would not be who and where I am today if it were not for all the people and experiences in my past (both personally and professionally). They have all helped shape me into the person I am today. Thank you to the Crisis Prevention Institute for not only supporting this project but believing that we could pull it off. Thank you to all health care workers (in the trenches and behind the scenes) for your tireless efforts in helping to manage the pandemic (COVID-19). You are all heroes.

Special Acknowledgments from Kim

I would like to acknowledge the multiple people in my life that helped make this goal obtainable. I am so thankful for their support and belief in my passion and work. I wouldn't be where I am today without them. Thank you to my mentors and managers that guided me over the years. You saw promise in me and encouraged me down this path throughout my career. Thank you to Susan Driscoll and to the Crisis Prevention Institute for all I've learned from you and for allowing me to share what I've learned as well. I'm overwhelmed by this chance to try to make a difference with WPVP at an international level. You continue to stand with integrity in this field. Thank you to my support system of family and friends, specifically, my parents and my brother and his family. Whether you helped proofread chapters, offered to listen to ideas, or checked in for ongoing updates, I appreciate your support during this chaotic and challenging time. To my partner Raj, I'm truly grateful for your love and support. There were many long hours and sacrifices made to make this book happen. Within the last 4 months of this project, I trained over 300 staff members at work, experienced a death in the family, attended a friend's out-of-state wedding, planned a family member's wedding proposal, celebrated birthdays for a niece and nephew, completed a full room renovation, experienced a medical setback, completed a large Go

Live for a work project, attended a First Communion, and had multiple other competing priorities. It was stressful to say the least, and you were there through it all. You graciously allowed me the time I needed to meet my deadlines and I'm truly thankful. Of course, thank you to Kyle. There's no one else that I would have preferred to write this with. You always bring a unique and valuable perspective and I appreciate your partnership. Lastly, thank you to all of our readers. Authoring this handbook has been an exciting adventure that has been a culmination of so many life experiences and opportunities and I'm proud to share these insights with my peers. This handbook has been a labor of love and I'm so grateful for this opportunity to share this important undertaking in this way.

Author Bios

Kimberly A. Urbanek has over 22 years of experience in health care and is a Master Level Instructor in Crisis Prevention. Kim holds a Bachelor's degree from Louisiana State University A&M and earned her license as a Nationally Registered Critical Care Paramedic from Loyola University Medical Center. She has held clinical roles in open heart surgery, critical care, paramedicine, and emergency services, as well as nonclinical and management level positions in Public Safety, where she developed a state-of-the-art Security Command Center. Kim has extensive experience as a certified instructor in a vast array of Public Safety and Emergency Preparedness areas (Active Threat, CPR, Crisis Prevention, First Aid, ACLS, Hazmat, Oleoresin Capsicum, JPX Defender, Advanced Physical Skills, self-defense, service recovery, Interview and Interrogation, Taser, etc.) and serves as a workplace violence prevention expert and specialist. Currently, Kim works as the System Manager, Administration and Training of Public Safety at Edward-Elmhurst Health, where she works to educate on and enhance the workplace violence prevention program.

Kyle J. Graham, CYCP (Cert.) Specialized Hon. Psychology has over 25 years of experience in academic research hospitals including The Hospital for Sick Children (Toronto, ON) and McMaster Children's Hospital (Hamilton, ON). Kyle is a Master Level Instructor in Crisis Prevention (holding certificates in Advanced Physical Skills and Trauma) and is a Certified Joint Health and Safety Member (approved by the Chief Prevention Officer, Ministry of Labor in Ontario, Canada).

Kyle has continued his education/training at a variety of universities in-cluding University of Toronto, McMaster University, York University, and Harvard School of Business. Kyle is passionate about creating sustain-able business/training practices regarding patient/staff safety and has consulted for many private and public institutions across North Amer-ica. Currently, Kyle is a Clinical Manager for the Child and Youth Mental Health Programs at McMaster Children's Hospital.

Contributor Bios

Dr. Lindsey Harrington is a Licensed Clinical Psychologist for Edward-Elmhurst Health. She served as a pioneer Employee Support Coordinator providing emotional support, mental health education, leadership consultation, and crisis debriefing to staff. She is trained in critical incident stress management and frequently works with hospital staff during behavioral and medical emergencies to help with de-escalation coaching and support. She has presented on topics including verbal de-escalation, defusing anger, emotion regulation interventions, and communication skills.

Ravi Hookoom is a Canadian Registered Safety Professional (CRSP) holding a BASc in Public and Occupational Health, a Certificate in OHS from Ryerson University, and an MBA specializing in OHS Leadership from the University of Fredericton. Ravi has over 20 years of practical experience in both Public and Occupational Health and Safety. Ravi currently works as a Safety Specialist at McMaster Children's Hospital, Hamilton, Ontario, Canada.

Erica Howard is a trained Occupational Therapy Assistant, with over 24 years' experience in the mental health field. She received her CPI Instructor certification in 2013 and is currently the Program Manager for the Prevention and Early Intervention Safety Training Program at St. Joseph's Health care Hamilton. In this role, Erica drives the crisis prevention and intervention training for the organization, focusing on postvention strategies and support for staff after a critical incident.

Katarina Kemper has been in the health care industry for over 20 years working in quality, risk, safety, security, and emergency preparedness. She is an active member of ACHE, ASIS, and IAHSS and participates in Women in Security groups. She has a BS in criminal justice, MS in organizational leadership, and a PhD in organizational development and change (grad. 2022).

Laura Larkin is a certified clinical nurse specialist and holds an Advanced Practice Nursing degree from St. Xavier University. She has over 30 years of nursing experience, which includes critical care and inpatient quality roles. She specializes in program development and implementation to meet strategic goals. Currently, Laura works in Ambulatory Care, embedding workplace violence initiatives at Edward-Elmhurst Health.

Deb Somers-Larney graduated from the U.S. Military Academy at West Point and earned a Master's in Public Administration from the University of Illinois at Chicago. She held a Top Secret clearance with SCI and is a Certified Protection Professional, board certified in Security Management. She has served in the Army, the FBI, and most recently as the System Vice President for Security for Advocate Aurora Health where she established their centralized security program and security command center.

CHAPTER 1

Workplace Violence in the Health Care Industry—An Introduction

CPI

Kimberly A. Urbanek and Kyle J. Graham

Objectives

After reading this chapter, one should be able to:

- Understand the growing epidemic of workplace violence (WPV) worldwide
- Understand the current demand for prevention efforts in health care
- Identify the reasons why prevention efforts are often not effective in health care
- Know how to successfully chart a path forward
- Understand the five ways this handbook is different from all others in how it will improve WPV programs

Workplace violence (WPV) is not a new trend. However, due to the growing number of incidents year after year, the awareness of "just how bad it is" continues to grow. And the growth is not small. There is a rapid surge of violence occurring in all workplaces, in both verbal and physical incidents, across the globe. Unfortunately, the health care industry has not escaped that swell unharmed. Health care areas are experiencing abuse like never before, and there is an increasing demand for safety and prevention efforts. This handbook, which was designed specifically for the health care industry, not only will outline the essentials of a WPV program, but will also provide new, updated ideas and solutions to violence in health care. This handbook will explore the current trends and address how to navigate WPV in all health care programs.

Violence Trends in Health Care

Violence in health care continues to expand, not just in the number of incidents and injuries, but also across all settings and disciplines in the health care arena. It is well known that there has been a historical propensity for violence in the emergency departments (EDs) and mental health/behavioral health areas. But there was never an overabundance of concern about violence in other areas. Cardiac units, dental offices, rehab facilities, doctors' offices, residential facilities, and **diagnostic centers** were never the headlining locations of concern. That does not necessarily mean that violence did not exist in those locations, but it surely was not a major source of worry, and it definitely was not talked about. That is, until recently. Stories are continually surfacing about unthinkable situations that are occurring in these "healing" environments. In April 2019, in Baton Rouge, LA (1), a patient attacked his nurse, grabbed her by the neck, and struck her head on a desk. She died several days later due to this assault. At Northeast Georgia Health System (2), a four-hospital organization, Public Safety calls to respond to protect a staff member from harm more than doubled between 2019 and 2020 from 349 to 711 incidents. And in Montreal, Canada, in September 2021, a nurse at a retail pharmacy was punched repeatedly in the face by a man, when he found out his wife had come in to receive a COVID-19 vaccine without his consent (3).

Over the last several years, incidents of WPV are increasing at frightening rates, and people and organizations are finally taking notice. The more prevalent these terrifying stories become, the more health care workers are finding their voice. Multiple awareness and change movements have been gaining momentum. Despite the known history of violence in EDs, it was not until 2019 that the "No Silence on ED Violence" campaign was started to address the staggering statistics of violence in EDs. The same year, after vigilant efforts of federal lobbying by the **Canadian Federation of Nurses Unions (CFNU)**, the House of Commons Standing Committee on Health conducted its first ever study into violence against health care workers. Many other initiatives have been in the works in recent years as well. The American Hospital Association (AHA) started "Hospitals against violence." The National Nurses United organization is lobbying for additional **Occupational Safety and Health Administration (OSHA)** mandates to require standards to address WPV. The Australian Nursing & Midwifery Federation (ANMF) (4), in partnership with the Registered Nurses' Association of

Ontario (RNAO), is working to "stamp out violence against health care professionals." They have been negotiating changes in legislation to enhance worker safety after a nurse was knocked unconscious, and almost killed, necessitating the use of cardiopulmonary resuscitation (CPR) to revive her. Recently, the World Medical Association (L'Association Medical Mondiale) defined WPV within health care as "an international emergency that undermines the very foundations of health systems and impacts critically on patients' health" (5). Violence in the health care world is now a known epidemic and, unfortunately, not one that is expected to go away anytime soon (Figure 1.1).

Simple Assaults 2012–2020

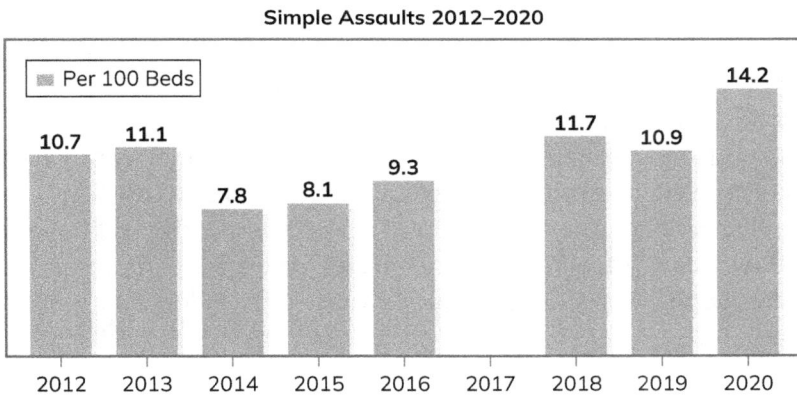

Figure 1.1: IAHSS Survey Results for Simple Assaults in Health Care (6)

Why WPV Prevention Efforts Fall Short

WPV issues have grown to epic proportions, and in response, regulations and guidelines have been created to reduce the number of injuries. Still, even though attempts to reduce injuries in health care settings have made slight improvements, prevention efforts have not been nearly as successful as improvements made in other industries over the years. So, why is this such a difficult issue to address in health care? Why have organizations' efforts not shown drastic improvements? There are multiple contributing factors:

- WPV is not built into the culture/not a prioritized strategic initiative
- Lack of effective policies and procedures
- Lack of staff awareness about WPV

- Lack of staff reporting/accurate data
- Lack of funding
- High staff turnover rates
- High-risk patient populations due to substance dependency, psychiatric disorders, chronic cognitive conditions, etc.
- Staff's insufficient de-escalation skills/lack of training
- Unsecured, open physical environments
- Extreme levels of patient and family stress/fear/pain
- Spillover from current events/societal and political issues

There are still many other contributing factors that make health care environments more prone to violence. The extensive number of variables makes combating violence a moving target in health care, due to the nature of the industry. With so many moving pieces, a successful program implementation may seem unachievable.

On top of the issues already noted, there are significant psychological impacts to staff, as well as to the patients and families in their care, due to this growing trend of disrespect and incivility. Employees are tired, burnt out, and even traumatized due to the repeat exposures to verbal and physical abuse. Recently, the CFNU identified that 61% of nurses expressed significant concerns with WPV, and two-thirds of nurses have considered leaving their jobs due to WPV issues. The CFNU goes on to report that the number of Lost Time claims has increased 66% over a 9-year period. Nurses and other medical health professionals are expected to work in, and respond to, high-stress situations on a daily basis because it is the nature of the work (7). *The American Journal of Managed Care* (AJMC) reported in December 2020 that most nurses and providers have been victims of WPV at least once in their careers and further describes the impact of WPV incidents and how they negatively affect the "delivery, quality and accessibility of health care" (8).

Psychologically traumatic responses can occur when staff are repeatedly exposed to these high-risk situations. It is known that traumatic WPV events are cumulative and wear down people's ability to cope (9), and this may result in increased symptoms of mental health disorders (10). In addition to the physical injuries that are sustained, it has been shown that a serious impact on workers' mental health has resulted as well, as revealed by a 2020 CFNU study (7). The study found disturbing rates of symptoms of mental health disorders emerging among physically traumatized nurses. Physical assault was reported as the most traumatic event, affecting 92.7% of nurses. Nearly half of nurses (46.4%) reported exposure to physical assault at least 11 times or more. The extent of the traumatic effects on these teams of health care workers still remains to be seen, but with the rising numbers that are being seen, an immediate solution must be found.

It should be noted that even with these enormous percentages, there is absolute certainty that the number of WPV incidents is still grossly underreported. Getting accurate data is truly challenging. Organizations do not have a way to "measure" where they stand against other organizations, as WPV statistics are not openly shared between organizations. This information is usually quite private and protected, even within an organization, due to possible fear or shame from publicizing incidents. In the vast majority of cases, the public does not have a clue about the level of WPV issues that occurs in their local health care settings, unless there is a significant incident that becomes newsworthy. Even if organizations decided to be transparent with WPV numbers, it would be challenging to align the figures. It should be noted that, unfortunately, there is no national standard for how to define and track WPV data or to what level data needs to be collected. Lack of standardization across organizations makes it impossible to compare apples to apples. When collecting data, **categories of violence** are not easily defined, and data is not often collected in totality. One incidence of violence where a patient was restrained could potentially generate four separate trackable statistics. But how those statistics are collected is solely up to the organization.

Imagine This Scenario

A patient became verbally abusive to a staff member and threatened physical violence while attempting to **elope** from his room. Additional staff responded, concerned about the safety of the patient. As the situation escalated, the patient attempted to hit a responding team member and actually spat on and kicked a third team member. The patient ended up being restrained and medicated.

So how does this data get collected? At a high level, this incident gets reported and documented as a restraint (Stat #1). However, an investigation of the details reveals that there was verbal abuse (Stat #2), a near-miss due to an attempted strike (Stat #3), an exposure from the spitting (Stat #4), and an actual employee injury (Stat #5). Based on the organization, this incident may count only as a restraint or as one event of violence due to the physical strike. Or it might be recorded as two incidents, once for the verbal abuse and once for the physical abuse. Or should all five pieces of data be recorded and tracked as WPV statistics? Stats may be different if collected by Public Safety, Risk Management, or Occupational Health staff depending on the goal. None of the data is standardized, which creates challenges and variance.

Based on the example outlined above, it is easy to see how reporting can quickly get complicated, even if you are able to capture all of the details. Further, when trying to measure incidents across a region or state or province, none of the data lines up to give an accurate picture, due to the vast differences in data tracking. When incidents are not reported and data is incomplete, or kept secret, it becomes extremely challenging for an organization to successfully fix or even troubleshoot WPV issues when they are unable to even understand the magnitude of the problem.

Charting a Path Forward

So, how can an organization even begin to chip away at the large and changing landscape of violence prevention? The idea of even broaching the subject of WPV can sound overwhelming, daunting, expensive, and exhausting. The good news is that there is definitely a path forward.

For organizations committed to making a positive impact with **workplace violence prevention (WPVP)** efforts, it is imperative that they are open to the idea of a cultural shift. An "all-in" type of approach will be essential in order to see success in reducing WPV incidents, but it can be done. It can happen incrementally and should start with reflecting on what is already in place. Use some creativity when reimagining how to build up prevention efforts. Organizations should realize they are not alone in these efforts. Connect and network with other organizations in the industry. Remove the stigma and bias that may exist around the current WPV situation. Be willing to relinquish antiquated ideas and have an open, renewed mindset, and explore the idea of continuous improvement. Remove the cloud of shame that may inhibit an exploration of what is actually going on in the organization and areas where deficits exist. Embrace the idea of transparency and collaboration so that successes and failures can be shared, to learn how to move forward as an industry. Train teams to feel empowered to identify and safely manage security concerns proactively. Champion the efforts, and do not back down from the struggles. Staff will gain confidence when they see that WPVP is a significant priority for the organization and when they hear and feel its importance echoed across leadership. This is an achievable goal, and even short strides can make a difference!

Using This Handbook to Improve WPVP Programs

This handbook was developed to serve as a comprehensive resource to establish and build out the necessary components of a successful WPV program. However, there are already plenty of existing regulations and guidelines on what a WPVP program should entail. So how is this book different?

There are five characteristics of this handbook that set it apart from others:

1.   This handbook draws from several leading WPV subject matter experts and incorporates years of health care experience across North America to provide the most up-to-date, current WPVP strategies and challenges. The ideas, plans, and best practices encompassed here have been tested and vetted by professionals in the industry who have first-hand knowledge of what does and does not work.

2.   This handbook is specific to the health care industry. This includes not only hospitals but all other health care entities as well. No other existing guidelines provide a comprehensive approach for all health care establishments regarding building a

WPV program. There is no other resource that demonstrates how to apply some of these tried-and-true hospital initiatives to the ambulatory and alternate care sites. That effort is long overdue and can no longer be neglected, because these sites make up most of the institutions in the health care industry. This handbook covers all types of health care organizations, regardless of size, location, or classification.

3. This WPVP plan is intended to meet an organization "where they are," representing an approach not offered by any other resource. Other resources broadly indicate where you need to go, without telling you how to get there. This handbook uses a "how to" approach that addresses an organization's need regardless of its starting point. In other words, an organization that has barely started developing their WPV program, as well as one that already has a fully functioning program, can both draw full benefit from this handbook. Learning how and why some initiatives are more effective than others is definitely a benefit. An organization can find small, impactful ways to begin building a WPVP plan or new ideas for program expansion, creative best practices, and documentation templates to round out their already robust program. This tool is designed to help determine where the stopgaps are and work toward developing them into permanent solutions. Even the very best WPVP programs can benefit from new and creative ways to sustain their progress.

4. Each chapter of this handbook is meant to stand alone. Given how different every organization is, an organization's approach to implementing this plan will vary from place to place. It is likely that most, if not all, health care organizations already have *some* pieces of a WPVP program in place. However, very few entities truly have *all* of the pieces in place, functioning at the highest level of efficacy. Thus, this book is intended to enhance and complement your current WPV program. A reader can explore this handbook from cover to cover or can simply zero in on a chapter or two to improve deficiencies that were identified in their organization. This resource is intended to serve as an aid for any job role or job title to develop the essentials of building a complete program.

5. This handbook will be a living document that gets updated and renewed regularly, growing and changing as the industry changes. The plethora of dynamic variables in health care make it necessary to amend and adjust strategies, approaches, and best practices over time in order to stay current and relevant to the end goal. WPV is an all-encompassing, ever-growing, ever-evolving issue. There will continue to be learning opportunities and pain points, and as more is learned, more will be shared. This handbook will allow organizations the opportunity to learn from others' successes and mistakes, to witness transparency in unprecedented ways, and to redefine what programs should consist of and look like. This handbook will develop into a repository of tools and templates that can be shared and utilized to save time, money, and efforts, all while working to improve the overall WPV situation in the health care industry.

Authors' Note:

Thank you for taking this opportunity to gain some additional insight into ways and means of improving WPV practices in your organization. Your interest in exploring what this resource contains demonstrates your commitment to your teams, your patients, and your community. We welcome the opportunity for you to share best practices and creative new ideas to further enhance this undertaking. In the continuously evolving WPV scenario, we promise to try to find ways to clear the obstacles in your path, to help you on this critically important journey. There is strength in numbers. We can decide to break down **silos** and build collaborative relationships to be part of the development and creation of new standardized requirements and legislature. We can drive the necessary funding needed to allow full implementation of WPV programs. We can work to effect change in how we universalize data collection and sharing across regulatory agencies and shift the mindset as a group of experts living this reality daily.

So, as you and/or your team members work through this handbook, we hope you find value and inspiration, as you discover a variety of best practices and guidelines. Whether your interests lie in the basic structure of WPV committees, or in creating internal response teams in ambulatory settings, or in deriving value from debriefings, or in focusing on staff wellness, we hope you find what you are seeking here. Please glean all the information you can about empowering and training your staff and building a sustainable culture of violence prevention. An idea from even one determined individual can become a game changer for your organization. We admire your desire and drive to improve the morale and safety of your staff and providers. In turn, your investment is creating the most collaborative and healing experiences for your patients, and their families as well. Good luck with your WPVP endeavors! We look forward to working with you in the future.

References

1. Skene, L. 2019. "Nurse at Baton Rouge General Was Trying to Save Colleague before Fatal Attack, Warrant Says." *The Advocate*, April 16, 2019. https://www.theadvocate.com/baton_rouge/news/crime_police/article_9b905c94-60bf-11e9-a3d3-774d09fdf5e6.htm.
2. Nurse.org Staff. 2021. "Nurses Say Violent Assaults against Healthcare Workers Are a Silent Epidemic." Last updated October 11, 2021. Accessed March 14, 2022. https://nurse.org/articles/workplace-violence-in-nursing-and-hospitals/.
3. Reuters. 2021. "Police in Quebec Seek Man for Punching Nurse over Wife's COVID-19 Shot." *Thomson Reuters*, September 23, 2021. https://www.reuters.com/world/americas/police-quebec-seek-man-punching-nurse-over-wifes-covid-19-shot-2021-09-22/.
4. Australian Nursing and Midwifery Federation (SA Branch). n.d. "Preventing Violence in Healthcare." https://www.anmfsa.org.au/Web/Get_Involved/Stop_the_violence_in_healthcare/Web/Campaigns/Stop_the_violence_in_healthcare.aspx?hkey=eb8337e1-8876-4168-ae29-69d1ad77cc8d.
5. World Medical Association. 2020. *Agenda Item 3: COVID-19 Pandemic Response.* 73rd World Health Assembly, Ferney-Voltaire, France.
6. International Association for Healthcare Security and Safety Foundation. 2021. *Healthcare Crime Survey*, p. 6. December 2021. https://iahssf.org/assets/2021-IAHSS-Foundation-Crime-Survey52401-1.pdf.
7. The Canadian Federation of Nurses Unions. n.d. "Workplace Violence." https://nursesunions.ca/campaigns/violence/.
8. Watson, A., M. Jafari, and A. Seifi. 2020. "The Persistent Pandemic of Violence against Health Care Workers." *The American Journal of Managed Care* 26 (12): e377–9. https://doi.org/10.37765/ajmc.2020.88543.

9. Carleton, R. N., T. O. Afifi, T. Taillieu, S. Turner, R. Krakauer, G. S. Anderson, R. S. MacPhee, R. Ricciardelli, H. A. Cramm, D. Groll, and D. R. McCreary. 2019. "Exposures to Potentially Traumatic Events among Public Safety Personnel in Canada." *Canadian Journal of Behavioural Science/Revue canadienne des sciences du comportement* 51 (1): 37–52. https://doi.org/10.1037/cbs0000115.
10. Khamisa, N., K. Peltzer, D. Ilic, and B. Oldenburg. 2016. "Work Related Stress, Burnout, Job Satisfaction and General Health of Nurses: A Follow-up Study." *International Journal of Nursing Practice* 22 (6): 538–45. https://doi.org/10.1111/ijn.12455.

Glossary of Terms

Canadian Federation of Nurses Unions (CFNU) The Canadian Federation of Nurses Unions (CFNU) represents nearly 200,000 nurses and nursing students across Canada and in a variety of health care settings (www.nursesunions.ca).

Categories of Violence Categories of Violence can refer to the way that data is captured. It can be captured as Type 1, 2, 3, or 4; or as verbal versus physical; or as a single or multiple incident event.

Diagnostic Center A facility that utilizes specialized equipment or testing to determine the nature of a medical condition. Diagnostic centers can include radiology services, imaging services, nuclear medicine, and pathology and laboratory services.

Elope/Elopement To leave without others knowing or being aware.

Occupational Safety and Health Administration (OSHA) A large regulatory agency of the U.S. Federal Department of Labor that ensures safe and healthful working conditions for workers by setting and enforcing standards and by providing training, outreach, education, and assistance.

Silo A system, process, or department that operates in isolation from others.

Workplace Violence (WPV) Any act or threat of physical violence, harassment, intimidation, or other threatening disruptive behavior that occurs at the work site.

Workplace Violence Prevention (WPVP) A system of attitudes, strategies, practices, initiatives, and behaviors that work to stop and prevent any acts of threat, harassment, intimidation, or disruptive behavior from occurring at a place of employment

CHAPTER 2

Building a Workplace Violence Prevention Program

Katarina Kemper

Objectives

After reading this chapter, one should be able to:

- Understand the regulatory and accreditation considerations of a workplace violence (WPV) program
- Identify the basic anatomy and requirements of a workplace violence prevention (WPVP) program
- Understand the best practices and hurdles when implementing a WPV program
- Understand the structure, function, and potential impact of WPVP committees
- Know how to measure the effectiveness of a WPV program

Similar to building a house, building a **workplace violence (WPV)** policy and prevention program must start with the foundation. Many organizations have an understanding of the basics, but there are many components to take into consideration while building a robust program. An organization will need to establish a committee, a policy, and procedures that meet regulatory requirements, just as part of the basics. Then, an organization must evaluate the program that has been established to continue to develop all of its parts. Defining these essential pieces will create a solid foundation so a successful program can be established.

Regulatory and Accreditation Considerations

Canada and the United States have enacted **workplace violence prevention (WPVP)** regulations to protect the rights, safety, and well-being of employees. Both countries' regulations cover large and small entities as well as all types of health care entities and employee types. The effort of both countries is to identify/assess, prepare, report, mitigate, and respond to risk factors that increase the likelihood of WPV events to occur.

The Canadian government has established and published an outline for Workplace Harassment and Violence Prevention (943-1-IPG-104) for all employers. Each province has an Occupational Health and Safety Act that mandates specific requirements for a WPVP program based on the government's publication. The three aspects that an organization is required to have at a minimum, as outlined in the federal publication, are a health and safety representative, a WPV committee, and a policy committee. WPV regulations in the United States fall under the **Occupational Safety and Health Administration's (OSHA)** General Duty Clause (Section 5(a)(1) 29 CFR 1960.8) and recommend employers to implement a WPV program that contains five aspects: management commitment and employee participation, worksite analysis, hazard prevention and control, safety and health training, and recordkeeping and program evaluation (1,2).

WPV is a large and growing problem in health care and has the potential to adversely impact the overall culture of an organization. It can undermine employee morale, increase turnover rates, lower productivity, and degrade the quality of patient care. Therefore, having a WPVP program is essential.

Workplace Violence Potential Impacts

- Adversely affects victims
- Undermines employee morale
- Lowers retention/high turnover rates
- Lowers employee productivity
- Staffing resource availability
- Employees' rights
- Impacts patient care
- Violence produces a fearful atmosphere

The Anatomy of a WPVP Program

As mentioned earlier, the regulating agencies require several aspects to meet compliance. This section will highlight each area in further detail. While each component is important, it is imperative for the foundational aspects to be in place, prior to building upon the program with other strategies. Each of these aspects will be addressed in more detail in the following section.

Management Commitment

The basic foundation, and often one of the most overlooked aspects of the WPVP program, is management commitment and policies. Management often receives the same training as all employees or a modified shortened version. The individual responsible to implement the program should focus on providing an in-depth education session with management to include program components, current facility event data/trends, opportunities for improvement, and how management should support the program. Table 2.1 lists several management commitment recommendations and best practices. Management support will be essential for a successful program, so efforts need to start here. (For more information about leadership and middle management roles and responsibilities, please refer to Chapter 5.)

Table 2.1: Best Practices for Management Commitment

Recommendations and Best Practices	What This Means	Hurdles and Pitfalls
Ensure all leadership is educated on WPVP; ensure they understand their roles and responsibilities	• Educate senior leaders, directors, managers on the WPV program and how it impacts the facility • Provide facility data and examples of current incidents and efforts to mitigate events	• Limited/lack of accountability • Limited support and follow-through on action plans • Limited participation • Competing priorities
Appoint individual(s) to lead the WPVP program	Formally allocate a key individual to lead and support the program	• Individual has limited authority to support WPVP initiatives • Weak leadership style

(Continued)

Table 2.1: Best Practices for Management Commitment (*Continued*)

Recommendations and Best Practices	What This Means	Hurdles and Pitfalls

Develop a supportive environment committed to a nonviolent workplace; establish a policy for staff reporting without retaliation; establish a formalized process to implement strategies that address, respond to, and measure WPV	Implement these WPVP Committee(s) *[refer to Committee section]*:
	• WPV Committee
	  ◦ Manages overall program for WPV
	  ◦ Reviews incident/injury data presented from other committees
	  ◦ Determines education for staff on WPV
	  ◦ Implements WPVP initiatives and strategies
	  ◦ Creates and establishes policies for WPV
	• **Threat Assessment Team**
	  ◦ Committee that assesses known individuals who pose potential risk
	  ◦ Assess threats made to an organization or individual
	  ◦ Develop safety plans and responses
	  ◦ Make determinations about follow-up
	• **Internal Response Team (IRT)**
	  ◦ Team trained to respond to active situations of violence or escalation
	  ◦ Real-time response
	• **Safety Committees**
	  ◦ Assess physical facilities
	  ◦ Perform hazard surveillance rounds
	  ◦ Identify and mitigate risks
	  ◦ Implement action plans for facility
	  ◦ Review all the Occupational Health and Safety pieces (stats, injuries)
	  ◦ Determine trends, moderate for change to improve identified gaps
		• Lack of participation
		• Lack of follow-through
		• Recurring themes and events where people can become desensitized
		• Lack of staff education on how to utilize response teams

Support employee training	• Provide resources for facility, department, role-based training based on WPV risks • Set goals for compliance • Encourage wide participation	• Low training compliance or failure to meet goals • Failure to utilize training techniques • Budget considerations • Time considerations for nonproductive hours

Table 2.1: Best Practices for Management Commitment (*Continued*)

Recommendations and Best Practices	What This Means	Hurdles and Pitfalls
Implement systems of accountability	• Develop, implement, and communicate WPV policies • Support reporting of events and near-misses • Perform timely incident and near-miss investigations • Implement action plans	• Lack of employee and management participation in reporting and investigations • Cumbersome reporting process • Failure to complete action plans
Communicate the program, expectations, results, and actions	Routine touch points on program and initiatives (monthly): • Newsletters • E-mails • Blogs, internal website • Department meetings • Management meetings • Organizational campaigns	• Minimal communication • Lack of participation • Employee inability to articulate program or action plans

WPV Committee(s)

An active WPV committee is where an organization can bring the WPVP program to life. The size of an organization may determine how many WPV committees are needed. There may be only one WPV committee for an entire organization, or there may be one WPV oversight committee, with several subcommittees/teams from other buildings/facilities that report up to the oversight committee. In addition, it is common to have other organizational committees (i.e., Safety Committee, Compliance Committee, Engineering Group, etc.) that report to the WPV committee as well. To form the main WPV committee structure, organizations should include representation from Public Safety, Risk Management, Legal, Human Resources, Senior Leadership, clinical staff areas, and Social Services (3). The committee/groups should be tasked to initiate and brainstorm prevention strategies, develop risk mitigation action plans, and provide an outlet of communication where vital information and statistics can be shared and reviewed.

There are several types of WPV committees that should be considered when building a violence prevention program. An organization may choose to implement one committee to cover all responsibilities or may divide up responsibilities across several committees or teams to assess, prepare, and respond to threats. Each committee or group should have a written charter to outline their scope, duties, responsibilities, and performance metrics. The frequency of meetings for these committees can be scaled to the size of the organization, and the volume of initiatives and responsibilities that need to be managed. Table 2.2 outlines several types of WPVP committees and the specific demographics for each.

Employee Participation

There are multiple ways that an organization can build employee participation in WPVP efforts, such as through the use of employee surveys and leadership rounding. Conducting employee surveys is one method to engage employees in the WPVP program and prepare them for any necessary culture changes in their work practices. The goal of conducting employee surveys is to gain further insight about the type and frequency of violence in the facility, and employee perceptions of violence, safety levels, and prevention efforts. This input will further help to identify potential hazards that may lead to violent incidents and related "gaps" in WPVP processes and procedures. Surveying employees can also provide insight into issues they deal with daily related to violence and can solicit ideas and feedback about ways they think WPV can be addressed in their work area. There are several types of pre-made surveys that can be purchased and used (Culture of Safety Survey, Violence Prevention Climate Survey, etc.) or organizations can create a customized survey as well. Either way, organizations should work to repeat the survey on a regular schedule, utilizing the same questions. This allows an organization to establish a baseline and then easily track changes and improvements. Trending can be done to see how gaps are addressed.

Another opportunity to solicit employee feedback is through a **Violence Prevention Climate Scale (VPCS)** survey that consists of questions employees rate on a Likert scale (4,5). This survey is designed to assess perceptions throughout the facility to measure aspects that may expose employees to violence. The survey can be distributed monthly, quarterly, or annually. Results should be trended to identify opportunities for organizations to create action plans. Continuous survey results may show positive or negative effects of those action plans and can serve as validation of what initiatives are working well.

Table 2.2: Outline of WPVP Committees

Committee Name	WPV Committee or WPV Policy Committee	Threat Assessment Team (TAT) or Threat Management Team	Internal Response Team (IRT)	Occupational Safety and Health (OSH) Committee
Purpose	To create and establish WPV policies, initiatives, and strategies for an organization. This team also determines educational needs and identifies and assesses risk reviews and other injury and incident data and implements action plans.	To investigate and manage threats and determine risk to an organization or individual. This team will receive, validate, assess, and interpret threats to determine follow-up and overall risk. This team will investigate concerns prior to/immediately after a WPV event.	To respond to active situations of violence or escalation to remediate individuals in behavioral crisis. Also often called Behavioral Escalation Support Team (BEST) or Behavioral Emergency Response Team (BERT)	To identify and mitigate safety hazards and risks to prevent injury and illness on the job. This team will conduct accident investigation and conduct hazard surveillance to identify health and safety issues/gaps and develop strategies to make the work environment safe.
Committee Members	Senior Leadership (Chair), Public Safety (Cochair), Human Resources, Clinical Educators, Risk Management, Emergency Dept. Management, Mental Health Leader, Nursing Leadership and representatives, Legal, Critical Care, Patient Experience, Ambulatory Leadership, and Marketing (Consider Physician/Medical Director)	Risk Management (Chair), Public Safety (Cochair), Psychologist, Chief Nursing Officer, Risk Management, Patient Experience, Medical Staff, Social Services, Human Resources, and/or department representatives as needed	Clinical staff trained in de-escalation, mental health, and/or trauma-informed care, medical staff, clinical social worker, and public safety. Consider: Nurse Supervisor, Public Safety, Mental Health Advocate, Charge Nurse of Unit	Health and Safety Representative (Chair), Senior Leadership, Public Safety, Building Facilities, Human Resources, Employee Injury Coordinator, Quality Coordinator, Risk Manager, Engineering, and any other department representatives

Table 2.2: Outline of WPVP Committees (*Continued*)

Committee Name	WPV Committee or WPV Policy Committee	Threat Assessment Team (TAT) or Threat Management Team	Internal Response Team (IRT)	Occupational Safety and Health (OSH) Committee
Role	Develop, implement, and measure WPVP program, policy compliance, recommend and vet training programs, conduct hazard/leader rounding, review event data trends, oversee action plan implementation and effectiveness	Educates and promotes reporting, conducts assessments and investigations, implements response plans, creates and monitors safety plans, conducts after-action debriefing sessions to review, evaluates and initiates action plans, and supports victim advocacy	Provides de-escalation options and intervention assistance to individuals exhibiting behavioral emergencies, provides staff support, considers medical indications	Investigates accidents and incidents and makes recommendations for corrective actions; promotes reporting of incidents and near-misses; identifies, evaluates, and controls hazards in the workplace, manages data collection and tracks and trends data, provides overview to other committees
Meeting Frequency	Monthly	Monthly	As needed	Quarterly
Performance Measures	Decrease incidents and WPV injuries, decrease risk, increase preparedness, increase staff sense of safety	Reduction in risk, events resulting in de-escalation without injuries or use of force application, increase in staff sense of safety	Activations, safe and timely intervention, education, and consults, staff ability to de-escalate	Decrease in number of workplace injuries, increase in reporting

In addition, the **Management Safety Climate (MSC)** survey measures the staff's perceived level of management and supervisor commitment to worker safety (4,5). While supervisors and managers may believe that they are promoting and advocating for safe work environments, the actions of management may be perceived differently by their staff members. Identifying any gaps with management support allows the management team to make necessary adjusts. Both surveys, the MSC survey and the VPCS survey, can be combined into one document that can be distributed to staff for completion throughout the year. Tables 2.3 and 2.4 list the questions for both surveys.

Table 2.3: Violence Prevention Climate Survey and the VPCS Subscale

To what extent do you agree or disagree with each of the following statements?	Disagree very much	Disagree moderately	Disagree slightly	Agree slightly	Agree moderately	Agree very much
1. Management in this organization quickly responds to episodes of violence.	1	2	3	4	5	6
2. Management in this organization requires each manager to help reduce violence in his/her department.	1	2	3	4	5	6
3. Management encourages employees to report physical violence.	1	2	3	4	5	6
4. Management encourages employees to report verbal violence.	1	2	3	4	5	6
5. Reports of workplace violence from other employees are taken seriously by management	1	2	3	4	5	6
6. Abusive behavior is not tolerated at work.	1	2	3	4	5	6
7. My employer provides adequate assault/violence prevention training.	1	2	3	4	5	6
8. My employer provides adequate assault/violence prevention procedures.	1	2	3	4	5	6

(Continued)

Table 2.3: Violence Prevention Climate Survey and the VPCS Subscale (*Continued*)

To what extent do you agree or disagree with each of the following statements?	Disagree very much	Disagree moderately	Disagree slightly	Agree slightly	Agree moderately	Agree very much
9. In my unit, violence prevention procedures are detailed.	1	2	3	4	5	6
10. In my unit, employees are informed about potential violence hazards.	1	2	3	4	5	6
11. In my unit, there is training on violence prevention policies and procedures.	1	2	3	4	5	6
12. In my unit, information about violence prevention is distributed regularly.	1	2	3	4	5	6
13. In my unit, in order to get the work done, one must ignore some violence prevention policies.	1	2	3	4	5	6
14. In my unit, whenever pressure builds up, the preference is to do the job as fast as possible, even if that means compromising violence prevention.	1	2	3	4	5	6
15. In my unit, human resource shortage undermines violence prevention standards.	1	2	3	4	5	6
16. In my unit, violence prevention policies and procedures are ignored.	1	2	3	4	5	6
17. In my unit, violence prevention policies and procedures are nothing more than a cover-up for lawsuits.	1	2	3	4	5	6
18. In my unit, ignoring violence prevention procedures is acceptable.	1	2	3	4	5	6

Subscale	Items to sum
Subscale 1: Practices and Response	1–6
Subscale 2: Policies and Procedures	7–12
Subscale 3: Pressure for Unsafe Practices	13–18 (reverse score)

Note: High scores indicate a favorable climate for reducing violence and aggression. To reverse score an item, use the following conversions: 1 = 6, 2 = 5, 3 = 4, 4 = 3, 5 = 2, 6 = 1.

Table 2.4: Management Safety Climate Survey

Management Safety Climate Survey						
To what extent do you agree or disagree with each of the following statements? My supervisor ...	Disagree very much	Disagree moderately	Disagree slightly	Agree slightly	Agree moderately	Agree very much
1. Makes sure we receive all the equipment needed to do the job safely.	1	2	3	4	5	6
2. Frequently checks to see if we are all obeying the safety rules.	1	2	3	4	5	6
3. Discusses how to improve safety with us.	1	2	3	4	5	6
4. Uses explanations (not just compliance) to get us to act safely.	1	2	3	4	5	6
5. Emphasizes safety procedures when we are working under pressure.	1	2	3	4	5	6
6. Frequently tells us about the hazards in our work.	1	2	3	4	5	6
7. Refuses to ignore safety rules when work falls behind schedule.	1	2	3	4	5	6
8. Is strict about working safely when we are tired or stressed.	1	2	3	4	5	6
9. Reminds workers who need reminders to work safely.	1	2	3	4	5	6
10. Makes sure we follow all the safety rules (not just the most important ones).	1	2	3	4	5	6
11. Insists that we obey safety rules.	1	2	3	4	5	6
12. Says a "good word" to workers who pay special attention to safety.	1	2	3	4	5	6
13. Is strict about safety at the end of the shift, when we want to go home	1	2	3	4	5	6
14. Spends time helping us learn to see problems before they arise.	1	2	3	4	5	6
15. Frequently talks about safety issues throughout the work week.	1	2	3	4	5	6
16. Insists we wear our protective equipment even if it is uncomfortable.	1	2	3	4	5	6

Violence Prevention Climate Scale Scoring Instructions

To score the VPCS 18-item version, sum responses to each item for the particular subscale as shown in Table 2.3.

Leadership rounding provides an immediate pulse point to gain a better understanding of day-to-day safety perceptions of employees. Leadership rounding consists of leaders soliciting feedback from employees as to their experiences. Table 2.5 lists some best practices for Employee Commitment. Leaders should consider developing a rounding card with standardized questions to track and trend responses over time. The questions may include:

- Have you experienced any WPV event(s) within the past week?
- Did you report the event(s) to Supervisor/Public Safety/other)?
- What went well during the WPV event? (training, response, recovery)
- What could have been improved upon? Was there any follow up action taken?
- Did your supervisor provide you support during or after the event?
- Would you like to use support resources (employee assistance program [EAP])?

Table 2.5: Best Practices for Employee Commitment

Recommendations and Best Practices	What This Means	Hurdles and Pitfalls

Solicit employee and management feedback	• Violence Prevention Climate survey
	• Management Prevention Climate survey
	• Employee Engagement survey
	• Culture of Safety survey
	• Touchpoint survey
		• False-positive scores
		  • Add "challenge questions" to validate that individuals are reading the questions
		  • Employees intentionally put high scores to prevent doing action plans or changes
		  • Must use same questions each time to establish patterns and identify trends

Participation in safety hazard assessments and action plans	• Employees participate in conducting safety hazard assessments and assist in developing action plans to mitigate findings	• Lack of employee knowledge • Employees failing to identify/ignoring issues • Employees identifying issues but do not help resolve them

Table 2.5: Best Practices for Employee Commitment (*Continued*)

Maintain a safe environment and report incidents or risks	• Employees report all WPV incidents • Employees follow appropriate de-escalation protocols • Employees remove nonessential objects/items	• Time to report incidents • Employee fear of retaliation • Employees not skilled in de-escalation • Employees failing to identify issues
Participate in committees	• Employees actively participate providing ideas, suggestions, and assist in mitigating risks	• Low participation • Low engagement • Lack of time • Time is not compensated

Worksite Analysis and Hazard Prevention and Control

Worksite analysis identifies and evaluates workplace security hazards and threats of WPV in restricted, secure, and private domains. Some reasons that security hazards can occur are broken/outdated hardware or equipment, deviation in operational procedures, or bypass of security controls. Examples of security hazards can consist of propped open doors into secured areas, inability to identify visitors or suspicious individuals, broken door locks, panic buttons not activating, or unattended ID badges with secure access. Formal and informal walk-though assessments of the environment to note issues, fix hazards, and educate employees on procedures will ensure a safer environment. The hazard analysis should also include how security technology is being utilized in accordance with organizational standards, policies, and procedures. Analysis of the results should be periodic and should occur at least semi-annually and whenever:

- new, previously unidentified security hazards are recognized,
- WPV injuries or threats of injury occur, and
- workplace conditions warrant an inspection.

Worksite hazard assessments can also assist the WPVP committee in understanding "gaps" and deficiencies. Assessments expand their understanding about information collected from the review of violence data, policy compliance, employee survey results, and action plan progress (6). Employees have knowledge and familiarity with facility operations, process activities, and potential threats for WPV.

Therefore, interviewing employees or conducting leader rounding during a walk-through hazards assessment may provide invaluable insight about hazard trends and procedural activities that increase the risk for violence in their workspace. Employees may also provide suggestions for physical environment and procedural changes that may reduce the risk of violence and/or improve response when managing violence. Table 2.6 lists several best practices for worksite analysis.

Table 2.6: Best Practices for Worksite Hazard Analysis

Recommendations and Best Practices	What This Means	Hurdles and Pitfalls
Worksite analysis by department and role	• Formal assessment of departments/ units that experience WPV events • Formal assessment of employee job roles that experience WPV events (i.e., nurses, technicians, security, etc.) • Formal assessment of physical building concerns/needs • Training specific to department/role	• Difficulty in completing assessments • Failure to mitigate risks after assessments • Lack of authority to hold departments/ units accountable for improvements • Funding to fix findings
Hazard prevention and control	• Conduct more frequent and less formal (informal) environmental and hazard rounds and mitigate risks immediately • Performed by unit staff in conjunction with committee members	• Failure to identify environmental risks • Employees failing to maintain a safe environment (i.e., doors propped open)

WPVP Training

Training is required to bring the WPVP program and policies to life. This component is one of the most critical components for employees. Organizations should provide robust WPVP training resources for at-risk departments, employees, and at-risk role-based positions based upon real-life events. General WPVP training should be conducted routinely for all employees, and those employees at higher risk should receive more focused or specialized training for mental health, de-escalation, and trauma-informed care (7). A determination of how to deliver training should come from the WPV committee. They should decide the content and who should develop and conduct this training with employees. Training programs should address the prevention, recognition, response, and reporting of threats, or actions of aggression and other behaviors of concern. The WPVP program should encourage and/or set expectations and goals for participation in training for at-risk employees or departments. (For more information about WPVP Training, please refer to Chapter 6.)

Investigating WPV Events, Reports, and Concerns

The WPVP program needs to include procedures for reporting incidents. This should include guidelines on receiving, interpreting, validating, responding to, and managing threats or violent events (3). All threats or acts of violence should be taken seriously and evaluated. Investigations may be initiated by a multitude of roles, depending on the organization. Public Safety, the Health and Safety Representative, the Risk Manager, the Quality Assurance Coordinator, or even a department director may be the appropriate party to initiate the investigation of an incident. Investigation should include events leading up to the event, facts, and witness information to assist in recommending appropriate actions. Investigations should be conducted as soon as possible or within the designated time frame, as identified in the organizational policy.

Employees that experience an event may need additional support. EAPs or Victim Advocacy Groups should be offered as a resource to employees to provide emotional support. These programs offer free and confidential assessments, short-term counseling, referrals, and follow-up services to employees who have personal and/or work-related problems (8,9). EAP or Victim Advocacy Groups help reduce workers' compensation, lost time claims, and health care costs, and address safety and security issues, improve employee productivity and engagement, and reduce costs related to employee turnover caused by the trauma of the event. Organizations can consider creating internal support groups as well, to show support for staff healing. Utilizing current mental health programs, chaplain services, or debriefing groups is also an option that an organization can put into place (Table 2.7).

Table 2.7: Best Practices for Investigating Reports of WPV

Recommendations and Best Practices	What This Means	Hurdles and Pitfalls
Initiate event or compliant investigations	• Review previous incidents • Visit the scene of an incident • Interview employees and witnesses • Examine the workplace for security risk factors associated with the incident, including any previous reports of inappropriate behavior by the perpetrator • Determine the cause of the incident • Take corrective action to prevent the incident from recurring • Document the findings and corrective actions taken	• Failure to report • Delay in investigation • Failure to gather all information • Lack of confidentiality
Offer or provide employee assistance through EAP or Victim Advocacy Groups (8,9)	• Offer or provide consultation and guidance to supervisors in dealing with employees who exhibit performance or conduct problems • Provide short-term counseling and referral service to employees • Refer employees needing long-term counseling to appropriate treatment resources • Help identify unsafe practices • Create additional resources for staff burnout/support	• Lack of employee willingness to seek help • Failure to support employee rights, privacy, and confidentiality

Record Keeping and Program Evaluation

Data provides a way for organizations to measure their performance and overall program effectiveness. Organizational data can be measured by benchmarking the facility's data against other facility, state, and national rates. Raw number data alone can be misconceived without the proper context, so programs should consist of rates relative to other comparable date. Some examples of **key performance indicators (KPIs)** and rates that should be monitored are:

- number of violent incidents/full-time employees
- number of violent incidents/patient days/department
- number of employee injuries due to violence/number of violent events

- number of violent incidents by day of week or by time of day
- number of violent incidents by employee

Organizations should collect and analyze data on a routine basis and need to report findings and trends to the WPV committee(s). Trends around violence will provide insight into determining patterns or anomalies. This data should be used to identify needs and what type of prevention training should occur and where. Once data is compiled, action plans can be implemented and measured to determine effectiveness of mitigation programs.

Measuring Program Effectiveness and Return on Investment

The **return on investment (ROI)** is a performance measure used to evaluate the efficiency or profitability of a program. The ROI measures the program value, relative to the investment cost. To calculate ROI, the benefit or risk avoidance (decrease of events or cost from previous quarter or year) of the investment is divided by the cost of the investment. The result is expressed as a percentage (Table 2.8).

Table 2.8: Sample ROI Calculation

Total Cost of:	Employee turnover + Medical malpractice claims + Employee injury claims due to violence/lost days or lost time + Cost of replacement staff
	divided by
Cost/hr:	Committee participation + Training compliance + Rounding

This measurement as applied to a WPV program allows an organization to evaluate the costs versus the benefits of the program. Measuring program effectiveness is important to assist decision makers to assess compliance, resources, impact, successes, opportunities for improvement, and ROI. This is a critical determination so that efforts can be directed to the most impactful and efficient initiatives. A successful WPVP program is important to have in every health care organization as it has the potential to adversely impact the overall culture of the organization. There are many data points that can be used to measure the effectiveness of the program. Some examples have already been mentioned, but others may include:

- Violent event rates
- Employee turnover rates
- Medical malpractice claims
- Employee injury claims due to violence/lost days or lost time
- Committee participation rate
- Training compliance
- Rounding, VPCS/MSC survey results/trends
- Employee satisfaction survey results
- Successful action plan completion

It can be difficult to determine the ROI of a WPVP program as the data needs to be collected from multiple areas and can take some time to obtain. However, when costs are totaled for all of the expenses that violence creates in an organization, it becomes overwhelmingly obvious how necessary it is to invest in prevention strategies. Presenting this data to the WPV committee and senior leadership teams demonstrates just how impactful an effective WPVP program can be. The ROI of reducing violence in the workplace can be an invaluable benefit to the organization.

Whether in Canada or the United States, WPV is prevalent in health care. Following the established guidelines allows an organization to truly make an impact with reducing violent incidents. By ensuring that all five aspects of a WPV program are addressed, an organization will be able to see the success of their investment. Organizations that are committed to WPVP create safe work environments for their staff, providers, and patients.

References

1. Occupational Safety and Health. 2016. *Guidelines for Preventing Workplace Violence for Healthcare and Social Service Workers. OSHA.* https://www.osha.gov/sites/default/files/publications/osha3148.pdf.
2. U.S. Department of Labor. "Workplace Violence Program." *US Department of Labor.* https://www.dol.gov/agencies/oasam/centers-offices/human-resources-center/policies/workplace-violence-program.

3. International Association for Healthcare Security and Safety. 2021. *IAHSS Handbook: Healthcare Security Industry Guidelines*. Glendale Heights, IL: International Association for Healthcare Security and Safety.
4. Hamblin, L. E. 2016. *Management Safety Climate and Violence Prevention Climate: A Mediational Model for Healthcare Employee Outcome*. ProQuest Dissertations Publishing.
5. Kessler, S. R., P. E. Spector, C.-H. Chang, and A. D. Parr. 2008. "Organizational Violence and Aggression: Development of the Three-Factor Violence Climate Survey." *Work & Stress* 22 (2): 108–24. https://doi.org/10.1080/02678370802187926.
6. American Society for Healthcare Risk Management. "Workplace Violence Toolkit." *ASHRM*. https://www.ashrm.org/sites/default/files/ashrm/Workplace-Violence-Tool.pdf.
7. CDC/National Institute of Occupational Safety and Health. "CDC/National Institute of Occupational Safety and Health." *The Joint Commission*. https://www.jointcommission.org/resources/patient-safety-topics/workplace-violence-prevention/cdcnational-institute-of-occupational-safety-and-health/.
8. Society for Human Resource Management. "What Is an Employee Assistance Program (EAP)?" *SHRM*. https://www.shrm.org/resourcesandtools/tools-and-samples/hr-qa/pages/whatisaneap.asp.
9. Society for Human Resource Management. "Understanding Workplace Violence Prevention and Response." *SHRM*. https://www.shrm.org/resourcesandtools/tools-and-samples/toolkits/pages/workplace-violence-prevention-and-response.aspx.

Glossary of Terms

Internal Response Team (IRT) A team within an organization trained to respond to active situations of violence or escalation to remediate individuals in behavioral crisis. Also often called: Behavioral Escalation Support Team (BEST) or Behavioral Emergency Response Team (BERT) or "Code Gray" or "Code White."

Key Performance Indicators (KPIs) A quantifiable measurement of performance over time for a specific objective. KPIs provide targets for teams to shoot for, milestones to gauge progress, and insights that help people across the organization make better decisions.

Management Safety Climate (MSC) Survey A survey tool that utilizes feedback from employees to inform a critical risk analysis of safety-related concerns across the organization.

Occupational Safety and Health Administration (OSHA) A large regulatory agency of the U.S. Federal Department of Labor that ensures safe and healthful working conditions for workers by setting and enforcing standards and by providing training, outreach, education, and assistance.

Occupational Safety and Health (OSH) Committee A team of people within an organization that identifies and mitigates safety hazards and risks in the workplace to prevent and minimize injury and illness on the job. This team will facilitate training on safety standards, review current safety issues, conduct accident investigations, and perform hazard assessments to identify health and safety issues/gaps and develop strategies and recommendations to make the work environment safe.

Return on Investment (ROI) A performance measure used to evaluate the efficiency or profitability of a program. ROI measures the program value or benefits, relative to the investment costs.

Threat Assessment Team (TAT) A team or committee that convenes to assess a WPV incident or threat to coordinate an organizational response in a unified and efficient way. (For example, if a patient threatens a nurse, the team will decide if the threat is significant and how best to counter it. They will gather facts like the patient's medical and mental diagnoses, current stressors, ability to cause harm, weapon ownership, circumstances that triggered the threat, and whether they have previous incidents, to decide an appropriate response.)

Violence Prevention Climate Scale (VPCS) A survey tool to assess individual staff perceptions of the extent to which organization management creates a climate that helps discourage employee exposure to physical violence and verbal aggression.

Workplace Violence (WPV) Any act or threat of physical violence, harassment, intimidation, or other threatening disruptive behavior that occurs at the work site.

Workplace Violence Prevention (WPVP) A system of attitudes, strategies, practices, initiatives, and behaviors that work to stop and prevent any acts of threat, harassment, intimidation, or disruptive behavior from occurring at a place of employment.

CHAPTER 3
Workplace Violence Internal Response and Follow-Up

Erica Howard

CPI

Objectives

After reading this chapter, one should be able to:

- Determine staff expectations during a crisis situation
- Create an Internal Response Team (IRT) to respond to active incidents
- Identify the necessary steps of what happens during and after a workplace violence (WPV) incident
- Identify the types of debriefings and necessary postvention procedures for staff
- Create a plan for staff support and follow-up post incident

---

An incident of **workplace violence (WPV)** can take on many forms and have different impacts on those involved in the crisis. Staff responses can range from needing a few minutes off the floors to experiencing longer term traumatic impacts from violent or abusive incidents. In an effort to better handle and reduce violence, organizations should provide response teams and other resources that are available to staff during or after an active incident. Ensuring staff are trained in how to summon additional support, when to activate a call for help (alerting an **Internal Response Team [IRT]**), and what their role is during a crisis, is imperative to everyone's safety. Staff must also have a clear understanding of what resources are available to support them post crisis and how to access these resources. Knowing when and how to call for assistance and reinforcing the importance of debriefing a situation will also play a vital role in maintaining staff's overall well-being.

Staff Expectations during a Crisis

There is a long-standing belief in health care that verbal abuse "comes with the territory." Although incidents of verbal/physical violence or abuse may occur in the workplace, that does not mean that it should be tolerated by staff. Staff need to be familiar with policies and procedures related to WPV which includes how to activate an internal response, clear guidelines on managing a crisis safely, and steps to follow after a violent incident has occurred. They must also have a clear understanding of the various levels of support that may be available to them. An organization's safety training program should include a review of policies and procedures that are relevant to staff's roles and responsibilities during the crisis, as well as how to access and implement these. It is helpful to choose a training program that focuses not just on crisis intervention but also on crisis prevention. This allows staff to learn and become skilled at identifying when an individual is in crisis so they can implement strategies that will help to de-escalate the situation before it leads to physical violence (1). (Refer to Chapter 6 for more information on training.)

When an individual begins to experience symptoms of anxiety or distress, it is imperative that staff recognize this and intervene as soon as possible. Staff should be trained to watch for noticeable changes or increases in behaviors that may be signs of distress. Individuals need support at this level. Simple interventions such as moving the person to a quiet space, offering comfort items such as water or a comfortable chair to sit in, and continuing to engage with the individual in a calm tone and manner can reassure the person and proactively prevent further escalation. As the person's level of distress increases, staff may need to take a more active approach in attempting to de-escalate the situation by using a firm tone when engaging with the person in crisis and providing clear directions regarding their behaviors. Staff should continue to use verbal de-escalation skills and strategies throughout the interaction and may choose to alert other staff in the area, asking for support and/or assistance with the person in crisis.

During a time of crisis, a person's ability to think rationally may be diminished, which can lead them to make irrational statements or threats of harm to staff or others. It is difficult to know what actions someone might be capable of acting on, so when staff are being threatened, they should:

- Stay calm and communicate in an even tone and manner.
- Attempt verbal de-escalation strategies in an effort to calm the person in crisis.
- Keep a safe distance away from the person to avoid being physically assaulted.
- If things begin to escalate further, staff should remove themselves from the situation as quickly as possible and seek further assistance from other staff, the IRT, **Public Safety**, or even police if necessary.
- Do not attempt a hands-on approach with a person who is an active threat, unless required by your role and trained to do so.

Internal Response Teams

Hearing an emergency call for help from a peer may evoke feelings of urgency and anxiety, as it indicates that someone may be out of control, and staff need immediate help. One way to prepare for these situations is for an organization to establish an IRT. An IRT is a team of staff within an organization that is trained to respond to active situations of violence or escalation to remediate individuals in behavioral crisis. An IRT may be part of a **Threat Assessment Team (TAT)** or may be a separate team from the TAT. These IRTs are often activated by a code word such as "Code White," "Code Gray," "Behavioral Escalation Support Team" (BEST), or "Behavioral Emergency Response Team" (BERT). There is no standardization of what to call the IRT so the name and structure of these teams can vary depending on each organization. (Refer to Chapter 2 for more information on committee/team structure.) There are several steps to establishing an IRT after the terminology is confirmed. Some of these steps include ensuring staff know when to activate a call for help, how to activate the IRT, who is involved in the response, and what everyone's role is during this potentially volatile situation. Being aware of the response procedure and being trained on how it works will help staff manage the anxiety that can be triggered during these events.

Activation of the IRT

As a situation escalates either verbally or physically, staff need to decide if further assistance is required and what level of assistance is needed. The first level of response may simply consist of communicating to other staff on the unit about a patient's demeanor (mood/affect, increased irritability, frustration, etc.). Pulling in other peers, unit specialists, or a charge nurse offers additional options when approaching the situation. Alerting others early on that there are concerning behaviors allows everyone involved in the patient's care to engage in strategies that may aid in avoiding a potentially volatile situation.

If staff are unable to resolve an escalating situation, they may choose to activate the IRT. There should be a variety of ways staff can summon immediate assistance. Organizations should have clear policies/practices in place and ensure staff know how to activate an IRT. Some methods of notification may include personal alarm systems/trackers, radios, phones, whistles, "Code" Buttons, unit-specific alerts, overhead announcements, or calling a predetermined emergency extension. The device/process should be loud enough to alert necessary responders that assistance is needed (2). When utilizing an overhead announcement as an alert, consideration should be used when deciding what to say as certain terminology may escalate the situation even further by causing the person in crisis additional distress. Regardless of the device or process used to alert, all staff should be trained on what specific method to use and what to do if/when they are alerted to an emergency.

Responding to the IRT

The members of an IRT may vary based on the organization, but typically should include a clinical leader, Public Safety Officers/security officers (if available), a patient advocate, and a mental health liaison (if available). An IRT could also be just additional peers or a physician/provider who responds to support the staff member in managing the active crisis situation. The makeup of this team will look different, depending on the organization. It is important to note that when multiple responders converge in a particular area, there is a need to have a unified, professional approach. Having the sudden presence of responders, or even the presence of a person in uniform may trigger a trauma response for the individual in crisis. To help mitigate this, upon the team's arrival to the unit, as long as there are no immediate safety risks, all responders should briefly huddle with the primary nurse to get updated on the current situation. This allows responders to partner with clinical staff to determine the type of approach and which interventions are most appropriate to be implemented.

Roles of the Responders

There are two basic roles that must be filled by members of the IRT, which are the Code Lead and the Code Responder (Figure 3.1). It is essential that one of the IRT members take the role of the Code Lead. The Code Lead helps define the strategy and approach and coordinates the actions of the responders during the incident. This lead role needs to be filled by a person who is confident and capable of effectively de-escalating a crisis situation and should be trained in crisis intervention strategies. If the situation involves a patient, the lead role may be assigned to a clinician who has the most rapport with the patient or who is familiar with the patient and their care plan. If the situation involves a visitor, family member, or another staff member, then the lead role may be assigned to Public Safety staff, or another member of the response team. The Code Lead is the only person who should be giving direction during the incident. They will initially brief the team and will be the main communicator to the person in crisis. The Code Lead is responsible for providing pertinent information to the responders and is in charge of leading the de-escalation, at least initially. It should be noted that it is a best practice to transition to a different lead if initial de-escalation efforts are not well-received. For example, if the primary nurse was acting as the Code Lead but has exhausted attempts to connect with the patient in crisis, one of the responders should assume the role of the Code Lead after being debriefed on the situation. Some of the details that the lead should brief the team on include:

- The circumstances leading up to the code being called
- If the person in crisis has any known communicable illnesses
- Special considerations such as any medical concerns
- If the person has a known history of trauma
- If the person has a communication disorder (hearing impaired or unable to communicate verbally)

Internal Reponse Team Activation

Code Lead

If the situation involves a patient, consider these roles to be the lead:

- Primary nurse
- Charge nurse
- Clinician with patient at time of IRT activation
- A response team member
- Public Safety/Security staff

If the situation involves a visitor, family member, or other staff:

- First person on the scene.
- Public Safety/Security staff to take over upon arrival

*Code Lead - ensures pertinent information regarding the patient is communicated to code responders, coordinates the code response with physician and unit staff, releases response staff when situation has been resolved, and leads the debrief.

Code Responders

Clinical staff that are part of the Internal Response Team or are assigned the role during their shift.

- Take direction from Code Lead or Public Safety staff
- Assist with verbally de-escalating person in crisis
- Assume the Lead role if directed to switch roles
- Clear objects out of the way (chairs, linen carts, meal trays)
- Direct others to a safe space away from where the code is taking place
- Engage in Holding Skills with person if required.
- Ensure readiness of **seclusion room** or **mechanical restraints** if being used
- Participate in the debrief
- Offer support to patients and/or family members who may be present during the code response.

Figure 3.1: Outline of Roles for an Internal Response Team

Other staff responding to the code will be assigned the role of a Code Responder. Code Responders must commit to following the approach laid out by the Code Lead and assist with safety during the incident. The Code Responders serve to support the lead. They can offer options as to how to approach the person in crisis and stand ready to assist with any needed actions. Some of the Code Responders' responsibilities include:

- Take direction from the Code Lead and offer support
- Monitor the physical and psychological status of the person in crisis
- Diligently observe and immediately speak up regarding any potential danger or harm to patient or responders
- Ensure that the area is clear of obstacles or dangerous items that can be used as weapons
- Be ready to transition to a lead role if necessary to take over verbal de-escalation
- Assist with physical interventions and/or ensure that others are using these skills correctly
- Call for additional internal or external assistance as required (Police)
- Offer ongoing support to other team members

The highest level of response may involve a call to police or 911. The decision to call police should not be taken lightly, and therefore it is imperative for an organization to have specific policy and procedure for staff to follow. The call to police should only be made after consultation with the Public Safety team and/or nursing leadership or management. Calls should be made through switchboard operators, Public Safety, or an internal emergency phone line instead of direct calls to 911 from a unit phone. Once the call has been made, the following guidelines should be met by staff:

- Immediately notify manager/site administrator that police have been called and are responding to the crisis situation.
- Once police arrive on-site, staff should provide as much information as possible to police regarding the person in crisis and the situation.
- Partner with police and take direction from them on what might be needed at that time.

It is best practice and an industry standard to have an IRT policy that clearly establishes expectations for the staff response. The IRT members should receive detailed, thorough training in verbal de-escalation, physical disengagement, and/or restrictive/containment skills. The training should also include any hospital-specific restrictive intervention options such as the use of seclusion, physical holds, **mechanical restraints** (such as the Pinel Restraint System) or the use of chemical restraint. Health care organizations may also choose to predesignate staff to be Code Responders to ensure that there are responders available on each shift. They should receive the necessary level of training to serve in this role. Staff may even be selected for this role based on their previous experience or skill (e.g., work experience, crisis experience, de-escalation experience), adding to their confidence and competence when engaging in a crisis situation (3).

Postvention Checklist

- Ensure that staff have not experienced any physical harm.
  - If they have, ensure they seek proper medical attention immediately.
  - Offer to accompany staff as they seek care and/or have staff accompany them to offer support during this difficult time.
- Support staff that may have a significant emotional response to the incident; crying or visibly upset, as they may need some time away from the unit to settle.
- Conduct a debriefing with everyone involved in the incident.
- Determine who needs to be notified regarding the incident:
  - Managers
  - Leadership team
  - Occupational Health
  - Staff's emergency contact, if necessary
  - Patient's family
  - Police, if needed
- Bring in additional staff, if necessary, so that staff involved in the incident can engage in self-care post incident.
- Offer a way home if the staff member is unable to remain at work for the remainder of their shift.
- When staff return to the unit, check in often to ensure that they feel safe and supported moving forward.

Figure 3.2: Postvention Checklist after a WPV Incident. Source: Crisis Prevention Institute, Non-Violence Crisis Intervention

*An organization may customize this based on their specific work environment and their post incident policy/procedure.

Postvention

The **postvention** process should include a number of components that will vary depending on the circumstances of each incident. This may involve a simple "check in" with staff to ensure that everyone is ok, allowing staff to take some additional time away from the unit during their break, offering comfort items or mindfulness techniques, or facilitating a formal debrief that may involve members of the leadership team (manager, director, executives, etc.). Regardless of the level of severity of the incident, postvention should include a standardized way to debrief with staff that were involved in and/or witnessed an incident of WPV. Organizations should develop policies/procedures on when and how teams should debrief, as well as how to access additional support for staff if needed. A checklist can be an efficient way to ensure that the necessary steps are followed, after an incident of WPV (Figure 3.2).

Types of Debriefings

Conducting a debriefing is an important part of the postvention process. Debriefing is a process to evaluate an incident and it's outcome to determine if the crisis response was effective. Debriefings are important to complete with the staff as well as the offender whenever possible, as it sets expectations going forward and can eliminate offenders from having repeat behaviors. Debriefings also address the physical, emotional, and mental well-being of staff after a violent incident. It is an opportunity to reflect on the incident in a nonjudgmental, supportive, and empathic manner. Details of the debrief, including who will facilitate it, what documentation is required, and when the debrief will take place, are all important questions to consider when developing a debriefing process. Investing in debriefings allows organizations to plan for better future interventions, enhance safety for everyone involved, and aid in preventing further incidents of WPV in the future. When developing your postvention strategies, it is important to first think about the different types of debriefings and when they should be used. There are three types of debriefings that will be discussed here:

1. Post Incident Debriefings—Occur immediately or as soon as possible after an incident (same day)

2. Process Debriefings/Outcome Reviews—Occur within a couple of days to a couple of weeks after an incident
3. Critical Incident Stress Debriefings—Occur initially within 3 days of the incident but are repeated as often as necessary and whenever needed.

Post Incident Debriefings

The first type of debriefing is often referred to as a post incident debriefing and should take place as soon as possible following an incident of WPV. This type of debriefing should be the most common and is typically a quick gathering that occurs on the unit immediately after resolving the WPV incident. This debrief needs to include the staff that were directly involved or witnessed the incident and can be completed within a few minutes. This debrief is essentially a verbal discussion to quickly review the incident. Staff can just verbalize this or can use a brief checklist or outline to prompt specific, consistent questions that should be asked. Either way, the debrief questions should be standardized across the organization. This post incident debrief allows everyone to do a quick "check in" with staff that were involved to ensure that everyone is physically and mentally able to return to their work. This post incident debrief should include the following questions at a minimum:

- Is staff ok? Any injuries? Mental or physical concerns before returning to work?
- Is the patient/visitor injured?
- What went well during the incident?
- What did not go well? What can be improved?

Staff may believe that they do not have adequate time immediately following the incident to discuss what happened; however, investing in debriefing is essential as it sets expectations for the offender as well as for the staff going forward. There can't be good prevention of further incidents if there is not good postvention. Taking a few minutes to connect with peers proves to be valuable for finding out what issues may have occurred and what follow-up should be done. In addition, if staff are not feeling emotionally ready to talk about the incident, it will be important as part of the debrief to provide them with additional resources. Addressing this as soon as possible can alert the team that there may be a bigger concern and can provide staff with a feeling of comfort and safety knowing that others are available to offer support as needed.

A post incident debriefing session can be facilitated by the Code Lead or someone in a leadership role, such as a unit manager or charge nurse. However, since these events can happen at any time of day, there may be times when management is not available to lead the debrief. Therefore, the debrief can be conducted by anyone on the IRT or by another clinician that was involved in the incident. It is important to ensure that staff leading the debrief are calm, fair, and capable of discussing the incident. They should be skilled at leading discussions around de-escalation, service recovery, etc. It may be helpful for these staff to receive training in topics such as de-escalation skills, Stress First Aid, building resiliency, and crisis management. They should also be familiar with WPV policies and procedures, and it helps if the staff member is respected by their colleagues as this may lead to staff feeling more comfortable when discussing the incident.

It is important to consider who to involve in the post incident debriefings. It may include everyone that was present during the incident, or just those that were directly and immediately involved. Staff who should be present may include clinicians involved in the person's care, as well as the patient's physician, and possibly support staff on the unit that may have been involved in the interactions with this individual. Although it is more likely to only involve those who were directly involved in the incident, it is possible that staff that witnessed the event may feel that they need some level of support as well. A post incident debriefing allows all involved staff the opportunity to share their observations and gain a greater understanding of the incident. The debrief of this situation may be quickly reviewed to ensure that everyone is safe, discuss the facts of the incident, and offer support and encouragement to those present. Once this group debrief is complete, anyone needing more support may remain in the room to further discuss the violent incident. Post incident debriefings can usually be managed at the unit level; however, if the incident resulted in a serious physical or psychological injury to a staff member or patient, or if serious errors were identified, additional debriefings may be required.

Process Debriefings/Outcome Reviews

Depending on the severity of the event, several types of debriefings may be employed. For example, if there was an unusual incident, or one that resulted in significant harm/trauma to staff or to a patient, a post incident debriefing or simple "check in" is not sufficient by it- self. Organizations will need to conduct a Process Debriefing/Outcome Review. A process debriefing or outcome review is a formal meeting that explores the facts of the incident and takes a deeper look at all of the actions that occurred. A Process Debriefing/Outcome Review should typically take place within a few days after the incident but could even occur up to a couple of weeks after an incident of WPV. This type of debriefing involves scheduling a time when the incident can be reviewed in detail, with all the necessary parties present. The process debriefing/outcome review is often facilitated by a member of the leadership team and requires some consideration to be able to include staff that were directly involved in the incident. Other members of the organization typically involved are Risk Management, Quality Compliance, Nursing Leadership, and unit managers. This type of de- brief involves a timeline review of the incident and specifically looks at events leading up to the incident, staff's response, outcomes for both staff and patient, injuries that may have occurred, process improve- ment strategies, and further planning for future interventions. This is a much deeper review of the incident and the staff response and should always consider how current policies and procedures may need to be clarified or adjusted. A process debriefing is beneficial in identifying gaps or deficiencies that occurred and often causes a review of oper- ations to see if a faulty process or procedure contributed to an unsafe situation. To gain the most value out of the process debrief/outcome review, it is critical to note that all shared information should be kept confidential and not be punitive or used for disciplinary measures. It will be essential for involved staff to be honest during this review, which will only happen when they are assured that it is a comfortable, safe, private environment for them to share.

Once it has been determined when the debrief will take place and who should be present, preparation should be done prior to the meet- ing to gather known information. A standardized model for the debrief- ing process should be used. This allows the organization to gather the necessary information to be discussed and reviewed, as well as any identified deficiencies that can be used to prevent future incidents of WPV. In order to proceed, everyone needs to be physically and mentally prepared to discuss the situation. It is important to open the session by reminding staff that this is a safe space for them to share their thoughts as this debriefing session is about gathering basic facts regarding the situation. Debriefing is not about finger pointing or blaming. These guidelines should be presented at the start of the session and staff must express agreement before proceeding. The staff leading the session should follow a set format that has been determined by the organization. If an organization does not have a debriefing template, there are several existing tools that can be incorporated. Crisis Prevention Institute (CPI), as a provider of Nonviolent Crisis Intervention® training, uses a tool called the CPI Coping Model to help facilitate debriefing sessions (see Figure 3.3). It may also be helpful to have a designated person to document during the debriefing. Accurate notetaking will be essential to capture the details discussed and any plans for improvement moving forward. To maintain privacy and confidentiality, the only information that should be recorded are the necessary follow-up steps that were identified as needing to be addressed.

CPI COPING MODEL	
Control	Ensure everyone is in physical and emotional control prior to starting the debrief. If staff need medical attention, they should be encouraged to tend to this prior to debriefing.
Orient	Review basic facts of the situation. What did staff see, hear, or notice before, during, and after an incidence of WPV.
Patterns	Are there patterns in the way that staff responded to the situation that should be reinforced? Are there patterns in the response behaviors that need improvement? Good or bad, these are important to identify to ensure future practices are improved.
Investigate	Identify alternate approaches. Should things be done differently? Are there better ways staff can respond or approach the situation? Are there alternatives to the disruptive behavior? Are there other response options available?
Negotiate	Get agreement on next steps and future responses. Set expectations to prevent recurrence. Learn from the incident and determine how to put it into practice in a way that ensures everyone's safety going forward.
Give	Feedback and encouragement are an important part of the debriefing process. Provide constructive feedback to each other, along with words of encouragement that will help to build staff's ability to intervene in the future.

Figure 3.3: CPI Coping Model ©

Critical Incident Stress Debriefings

A third type of debriefing is a **Critical Incident Stress Debriefing (CISD)**. In situations where someone has experienced significant physical or psychological trauma during an incident of WPV, it may be beneficial for affected staff to participate in a CISD with other members of their team. A CISD is a specific, seven-step process where a supportive, crisis-focused discussion is facilitated with a small, homogeneous group of people who encountered a powerful traumatic event. The goal of a CISD is reduction of distress and a restored sense of safety, group cohesion, and unit performance. While a process debriefing/outcome review is used to evaluate facts, process, and performance, a CISD is used to help staff digest the emotions and feelings surrounding an event. This level of debriefing is only led by a trained certified individual that will work with the staff to build resiliency and aid in recovery following a traumatic incident. Organizations may have trained mental health professionals on staff to lead this type of debriefing, or they may bring in an outside company to assist. A CISD focuses on how staff feel about the incident that occurred and how it's still affecting them, both at home and at work. Attendance at a CISD is completely voluntary and confidential. As a rule of thumb, no management staff are typically present during these debriefings to help set the environment up for more honest and raw sharing, without privacy and safety concerns. Again, the facilitator must emphasize the critical need for confidentiality during this type of debriefing. A CISD should typically take place within 48–72 hours after an incident has occurred and may actually be repeated a week or two later with the understanding that as staff process the event over time, different emotions or issues may surface. A CISD should include only those staff that were directly involved in the incident, and only those who choose to participate. This type of debriefing is not meant to take the place of other types of debriefings or conversations that may occur but is meant to be used in addition to a post incident debrief and/or other types of debriefings that may take place within the organization.

Documentation

The final part of the debriefing process involves documentation. The details that are discussed during a debriefing session allow organizations to identify plans for improvement in future interventions

(Refer to Chapter 10 for debriefing document template). This ensures better staff and patient safety, as well as allows for opportunities to make quality improvements and fix gaps. It is imperative to ensure that incident details are carefully and accurately recorded as soon as possible. Documentation may look different, depending on the organization. Various formats may be used and could be as simple as having an IRT/"Code" form with a checklist for staff to follow post incident, or could it be a more comprehensive incident report recording specifics about behaviors that were displayed and which staff responses were implemented and how successful they were. Regardless of the type of documentation, there are some key factors that should be considered when documenting WPV debriefings:

- Date/time of incident
- How staff were alerted to the incident (i.e., alert via a personal alarm device, IRT activated, staff yelling out for assistance, etc.)
- Names of involved staff/witnesses
- Patient information
- Brief details regarding the incident
- Injuries sustained by staff
- Injuries sustained by patient
- Outcome of the incident (patient placed in restraint/seclusion, patient medicated, patient successfully de-escalated, etc.)
- Factors that worked well during the situation
- Obstacles/things that should be done differently moving forward
- Plan for future interventions

Additional details to consider, if appropriate, include:

- Staff that are present for debriefing (if not confidential)
- Specific process details/timeline regarding the incident being discussed
- Required follow-up on pertinent issues

These pieces of information can not only provide a high-level overview of the incident but also allow organizations to collect data and reflect on what has happened, or if there is a need for a more formal process debriefing or CISD. Debriefing is a critical part of the postvention process following an incident of WPV because it can also highlight patterns of response and strengths or opportunities for staff. Not only does it allow staff a space to voice their perspective on the situation, it reminds them that they were not alone and that there may be others that are struggling in the same way that they are. Debriefings can create a feeling of unity through what can be a very difficult time for staff which can allow them to gain closure on the incident.

Staff Wellness/Incident Follow-Up

Ensuring staff's health and well-being should be a crucial part of your WPV response plan; however, it is also something that should be included in staff's daily routine while at work. Providing ongoing support and training to staff regarding resiliency, stress management, and effective self-care strategies can not only aid in building capacity in staff's ability to manage difficult situations, but it can also lead to lower rates of burn-out or compassion fatigue and increase staff's work–life balance. It is common for organizations to offer some sort of **Employee Assistance Program** (EAP) for staff. Unfortunately, staff often have no idea what services are offered nor how to access their EAP services. Information on staff resources and availability should be reviewed regularly during unit huddles or staff meetings so it is not just highlighted after an incident of WPV. Be sure to provide information on how to access EAP services, what type of support is available, and even some of the circumstances under which staff might want to reach out to an EAP provider. As part of this discussion, it is also imperative that staff understand that this service is confidential. Staff may choose to only access these services after they have experienced a traumatic event, so the more efforts are made to normalize these services, the more likely they are to access them and not feel embarrassed or judged (4).

Peer Support Program

Experiencing a traumatic event at work can feel isolating. Sometimes, the only one who can fully understand what that experience was like is someone that has been through a similar event. This is where an **Employee Peer Support Program** may be helpful. A peer can offer support by listening to the staff experience, can provide them with a feeling of security by being physically present for them, and can serve as a support system for them emotionally. When developing a peer support program, it is important to engage key stakeholders for program support, such as Occupational Health and Safety, Human Resources, and any other pertinent departments. Involving necessary departments allows the program to address essential logistics so that the program can be successful. Considerations when establishing a peer support program include proper selection of peer support providers, appropriate training, setting guidelines around use, and creating a psychologically safe environment. Organizations will need to provide thorough training around the parameters of what can and cannot be offered to staff that may reach out, as well as how to set these boundaries when speaking with staff that have experienced trauma. A rigorous interview process should be in place to ensure that those stepping forward as peers are appropriate for this role. It is also important to ensure that there are necessary supports in place for these peers, and that they have a private, safe space where they can debrief staff interactions. Multiple health care organizations have successfully implemented Peer Support Programs, so it can be beneficial to connect with other organizations to gain an understanding of logistics and pitfalls when developing a program.

A violent event of any sort can lead to a trauma response. Further, when this event happens at work, a place that was once a safe haven can become a place that triggers fear, anxiety, and trauma. Ensuring that staff are prepared to manage crisis situations is an essential part of preventing incidents of WPV and harm/injury should they occur. Building resiliency in staff goes beyond postvention strategies and needs to include ongoing support and encouragement while at work. Staff wellness practices should be embedded into the culture of the organization. Reminders about staff resources, a "Thank you" basket of treats from leadership, or routinely recognizing staff's efforts and success are all important ways to help staff feel appreciated and valued. It is important to recognize the toll that WPV can take on staff and work to do everything possible to prevent these incidents from happening. Organizations can make huge impacts by creating resources to support staff during an incident, ensuring follow-up is completed with affected staff, and, most importantly, ensuring that we provide support to staff on a daily basis. Violence can be unpredictable, but by creating IRTs to support staff during active incidents and by promoting staff's health and well-being, organizations are building a sense of safety and staff are able to effectively manage WPV incidents. Ensuring a safe space, time, and opportunity for staff to debrief with their peers and leadership can lead to staff feeling safer at work, and will build resiliency within the team, as well as improve response in future incidents (5).

References

1. Registered Nurses' Association of Ontario. 2008. "Position Statement: Violence against Nurses—'Zero' Tolerance for Violence against Nurses and Nursing Students." *RNAO*, August 31, 2008. https://rnao.ca/policy/position-statements/violence-against-nurses.
2. Ontario.ca. n.d. "Occupational Health and Safety Act, R.S.O. 1990, c. O.1." Part III.0.1, Violence and Harassment. Last modified December 2021. https://www.ontario.ca/laws/statute/90o01.
3. Registered Nurses' Association of Ontario. 2009. "Preventing and Managing Violence in the Workplace." *RNAO_Violence in Workplace*, June 2009. https://rnao.ca/sites/rnao-ca/files/Preventing_and_Managing_Violence_in_the_Workplace.pdf.
4. National Center for PTSD. 2018. "Stress First Aid Self Care/Organizational Support Model." *NCPTSD*, March 2018. https://www.theschwartzcenter.org/media/Stress-First-Aid-Self-Care-Organizational-NCPTSD10.pdf.
5. The Schwartz Center for Compassionate Healthcare, Boston, The Schwartz Center. www.info-trauma.org.

Glossary of Terms

Critical Incident Stress Debriefing (CISD) A specific, seven-step process where a supportive, crisis-focused discussion is facilitated with a small, homogeneous group of people who encountered a powerful traumatic event. It aims at reduction of distress and a restoration of group cohesion and unit performance.

Employee Peer Support Program A program that is established within an organization to support employees after an incident of WPV and/or trauma. It can effectively promote employee

resiliency and effective coping strategies to advance the psychological health and safety of staff. This program is meant
to be a nonjudgmental, safe, and supportive relationship between two people who have a lived experience in common.

Internal Response Team (IRT) A team within an organization
trained to respond to active situations of violence or escalation
to remediate individuals in behavioral crisis. Also often called:
Behavioral Escalation Support Team (BEST) or Behavioral Emergency Response Team (BERT) or "Code Gray" or "Code White."

Mechanical Restraints A device that is used to restrain the movement of the whole or part of a person's body. Restraints are
commonly used when an individual is displaying behaviors
that may cause harm to themselves or someone else.

Postvention An organized immediate, short-term, and long-term
response in the aftermath of a suicide to promote healing and
mitigate the negative effects of exposure to discuss the actions and thought processes involved in a particular clinical
situation, encourage reflection, and incorporate improvement
into future performance.

Public Safety A department in a health care system that has a
broad span of responsibilities, some of which include managing
safety and security incidents, responding to emergency incidents, de-escalating verbal and physical disturbances, assisting
with keeping patients safe, handling credentialing and identification of staff, and managing parking responsibilities. Sometimes referred to as the "Security" or "Protection" department.

Seclusion Room A space with a locked entrance/exit that is used
as a form of environmental restraint. This space is used to
confine a patient when they may be at risk of harming others.

Threat Assessment Team A team or committee that convenes
to assess a WPV incident or threat to coordinate an organizational response in a unified and efficient way. (For example, if a patient threatens a nurse, the team will decide if
the threat is significant and how best to counter it. They will
gather facts like the patient's medical and mental diagnoses,
current stressors, ability to cause harm, weapon ownership,

circumstances that triggered the threat, and whether they have previous incidents, to decide an appropriate response.)

Workplace Violence (WPV) Any act or threat of physical violence, harassment, intimidation, or other threatening disruptive behavior that occurs at the work site.

Workplace Violence Prevention (WPVP) A system of attitudes, strategies, practices, initiatives, and behaviors that work to stop and prevent any acts of threat, harassment, intimidation, or disruptive behavior from occurring at a place of employment.

CHAPTER 4

Gathering Data: It Must Be Measured to Be Managed

Ravi Hookoom

CPI

Objectives

After reading this chapter, one should be able to:

- Better understand current workplace violence prevention trends in health care
- Understand the need to collect data
- Understand which statistics to collect and track to ensure data quality
- Know how to utilize staff reporting to collect data
- Analyze data to evaluate and communicate potential risk
- Understand how to implement prevention controls
- Evaluate risks and prevention strategies for continuous quality improvement

---

Workplace violence (WPV) in health care is a widespread issue across the globe. Patients may get agitated if they feel they are not well taken care of, causing them to express their frustration toward health care workers. Since health care providers work closely with patients and their families, they are most likely to be subject to these aggressive behaviors. Many health care workers do not report such incidents because they feel it is an expectation of their job, or they do not have time. Not reporting only increases the incidence of WPV. WPV also effects patient care, leading to an increase in expenses. Organizations must address WPV to reduce the incidence, improve patient care, and improve the working conditions of health care practitioners. Completing a risk assessment of WPV and implementing the resulting corrective actions can better protect health care workers (1). This chapter will outline why organizations need to collect data, how to analyze the data, and applications of use for the data in WPV risk identification and prevention. Applications here refers to Occupational Health and Safety (OHS) programs or interventions.

The U.S. Department of Labor defines WPV as "an act or threat of physical violence, harassment, intimidation, or other threatening disruptive behavior that occurs at the workplace." OHS in the Canadian health care sector is governed by provincial Acts and Regulations. While each province has its own OHS legislations, they are very similar in content. The Ontario OHS Act defines **WPV harassment** and violence separately, such as "engaging in a course of vexatious comments or conduct against a worker in a workplace that is known or ought reasonably to be known to be unwelcome" (2).

Current WPV Trends in the Health Care Sector

The health care sector has been plagued with WPV incidents over the years. Many analysts, researchers, and leaders have tried to pinpoint the definitive causes of such occurrences and strategies to minimize them. In reality, there continues to be a constant increase in WPV incidents in the health care industry. In 2019, the health care sector in Canada had the highest number of **Lost Time (LT)**[1] claims in Canada (Figure 4.1) (3), more than any other industry.

In 2019, the U.S. Bureau of Labor reported 5,333 fatal workplace injuries caused by another person (4). This number went down to 4,764 in 2020 (Table 4.1). Although this is a slight decrease, note that there is still a significant number of injuries in health care, with 202,510 nonfatal occupational injuries and illnesses involving days away from work[2] (Table 4.2). The incidence rate of "non-fatal intentional **injury (I)** by other person" was highest in the health care sector, more than all other sectors combined in the United States (Figure 4.2).

---

[1]Total number of working hours or days that are lost because of injury. For Canada the day the injury occurred is not considered lost time. The remaining hours in the shift is paid by the employer. Any subsequent hours or days lost is accounted as Lost Time.

[2]Days away from work include those that result in days away from work with or without job transfer or restriction.

The psychiatric hospitals experienced the highest incidence rate on "nonfatal intentional injury by other person," per 10,000 full-time workers at a rate of 124.9 in the United States (Table 4.3). Figure 4.3 shows the workplace homicides to health care workers by assailant. When these numbers are extrapolated with the hours lost due to injuries, we note that the health care sector, a field that is already short staffed and stretched, experiences further staff shortages. This further exacerbates the operational capacity of health care facilities, which in turn can cause other injuries, due to physical overexertion and/or mental stress. Patient safety can also be impacted with overstretched human resources (5).

Some professions are more at risk for violence than others. The Bureau of Labor statistics state that psychiatric aides were subjected to the highest rate of violent injuries, resulting in days away from work. This rate is the highest among other professions within the health care sector. In 2013, the most common incidents across all health care professions were physical violence, such as kicking and beating (see Figure 4.4). In health care settings, patients are the largest source of violence. Visitors and students are among the other sources (Figure 4.5) (7).

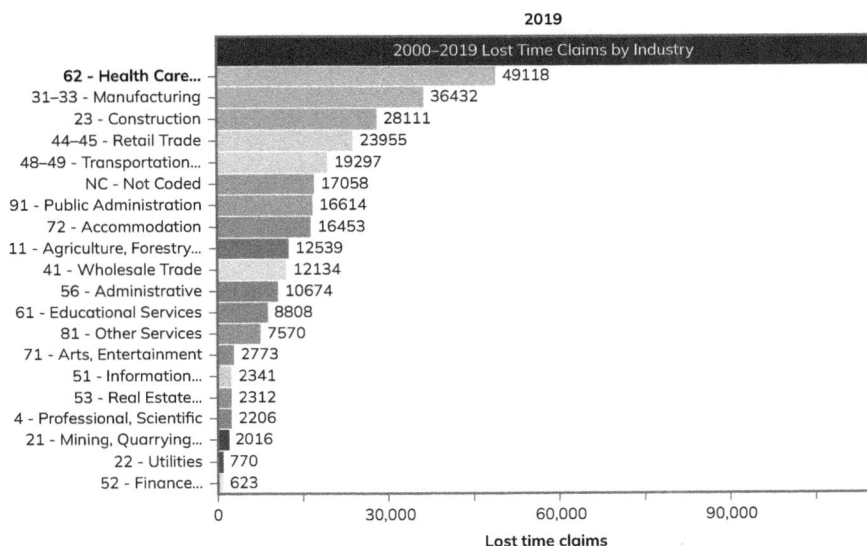

2019

Industry	Lost time claims
62 - Health Care...	49118
31–33 - Manufacturing	36432
23 - Construction	28111
44–45 - Retail Trade	23955
48–49 - Transportation...	19297
NC - Not Coded	17058
91 - Public Administration	16614
72 - Accommodation	16453
11 - Agriculture, Forestry...	12539
41 - Wholesale Trade	12134
56 - Administrative	10674
61 - Educational Services	8808
81 - Other Services	7570
71 - Arts, Entertainment	2773
51 - Information...	2341
53 - Real Estate...	2312
4 - Professional, Scientific	2206
21 - Mining, Quarrying...	2016
22 - Utilities	770
52 - Finance...	623

2000–2019 Lost Time Claims by Industry

Figure 4.1: 2019 Lost Time (LT) Claims in Canada (3)

Table 4.1: Fatal Injuries for Selected Occupations in the United States
(*USBLS n.d.*)

Characteristic	2016	2017	2018	2019	2020
Total[1]	5,190	5,147	5,250	5,333	4,764
Occupation (SOC)[2]					
Management occupations	377	396	387	380	361
Business and financial operations occupations	27	29	38	29	23
Computer and mathematical occupations	16	11	12	15	8
Architecture and engineering occupations	41	23	30	43	31
Life, physical, and social science occupations	15	13	18	15	17
Community and social services occupations	27	37	23	31	26
Legal occupations	13	11	15	11	5
Educational instruction and library occupations	32	30	27	24	13
Arts, design, entertainment, sports, and media occupations	64	47	71	40	36
Health care practitioners and technical occupations	60	57	65	56	51
Health care support occupations	30	28	32	38	44
Protective service occupations	281	266	270	231	229
Fire fighting and prevention workers	35	35	33	24	-
Law enforcement workers	127	117	127	97	115
Food preparation and serving related occupations	92	89	100	99	82
Building and grounds cleaning and maintenance occupations	329	326	350	333	307
Building cleaning and pest control workers	74	68	66	63	61
Grounds maintenance workers	217	191	225	229	202
Personal care and service occupations	55	69	63	61	58
Sales and related occupations	254	232	241	240	200
Supervisors, sales workers	104	98	102	99	73
Retail sales workers	102	89	99	96	95

Characteristic	2016	2017	2018	2019	2020
Office and administrative support occupations	78	101	69	92	69
Farming, fishing, and forestry occupations	290	264	262	291	264
Agricultural workers	157	155	158	183	148
Fishing and hunting workers	26	41	31	44	42
Forest, conservation, and logging workers	95	57	57	49	42
Construction and extraction occupations	970	965	1,003	1,066	976
Supervisors of construction and extraction workers	134	121	144	136	88
Construction trades workers	736	747	731	809	771
Extraction workers	41	41	64	50	59
Installation, maintenance, and repair occupations	470	414	420	438	393
Vehicle and mobile equipment mechanics, installers, and repairers	154	143	152	155	135
Production occupations	216	221	225	245	224
Transportation and material moving occupations	1,388	1,443	1,443	1,481	1,282
Air transportation workers	75	59	71	85	50
Motor vehicle operators	1,012	1,084	1,044	1,091	933
Material moving workers	228	235	255	238	218
Military occupations[3]	62	72	82	65	-

[1]The Census of Fatal Occupational Injuries (CFOI) has published data on fatal occupational injuries for the United States since 1992. During this time, the classification systems and definitions of many data elements have changed. See the CFOI Definitions page (www.bls.gov/iif/oshcfdef.htm) for a more detailed description of each data element.

[2]CFOI has used several versions of the Standard Occupation Classification (SOC) system since 2003 to define occupation. For complete information on the version of SOC used in these years, see our definitions page at https://www.bls.gov/iif/oshcfdef.htm. Cases where occupation is unknown are included in the total.

[3]Includes fatal injuries to persons identified as resident armed forces regardless of individual occupation listed.

Note: Data for all years are revised and final. Totals for major categories may include subcategories not shown separately. Dashes indicate no data reported or data that do not meet publication criteria. N.e.c. means "not elsewhere classified." CFOI fatal injury counts exclude illness-related deaths unless precipitated by an injury event.

Source: U.S. Department of Labor, Bureau of Labor Statistics, in cooperation with state, New York City, District of Columbia, and federal agencies, Census of Fatal Occupational Injuries

Table 4.2: Number of Nonfatal Occupational Injuries and Illnesses Involving Days Away from Work in the United States

Number of nonfatal occupational injuries and illnesses involving days away from work by selected worker and case characteristics and industry, All U.S., all ownerships, 2020		
	All ownerships	
Characteristic	**2020**	
Occupation:		
Management, business, financial	55,160	4%
Computer, engineering, and science	8,530	1%
Educational instruction and library occupations	39,020	3%
Health care practitioners and technical	202,510	14%
Service	472,990	33%
Sales and related	60,450	4%
office and administrative support	58,060	4%
Farming, fishing, and forestry	16,280	1%
Construction and extraction	81,430	6%
Installation, maintenance, and repair	89,330	6%
Production	114,430	8%
Transportation and material moving	223,930	16%
Event or exposure:		
Violence end other injuries by persons or animal	75,950	
Intentional injury by other person	37,060	
Injury by person unintentional or intent unknown	24,270	
Animal and insect related Incidents	14,510	
Transportation incidents	54,750	
Roadway incidents involving motorized land vehicles	36,670	
Fires, explosions	2,600	
Falls, slips, trips	256,830	
Slips, trips without fall	37,070	
Fall on same level	158,390	

	All ownerships
Characteristic	**2020**
Fall to lower level	56,160
Exposure to harmful substances or environments	491,190
Contact with object, equipment	222,240
Struck by object	126,010
Struck against object	51,110
Caught in object, equipment, material	31,630
Overexertion and bodily reaction	312,700
Overexertion in lifting or lowering	93,740
Repetitive motion involving microtasks	18,790
All other	8,300

Number of nonfatal occupational injuries and illnesses involving days away from work by selected worker and case characteristics and industry, All U.S., all ownerships, 2020

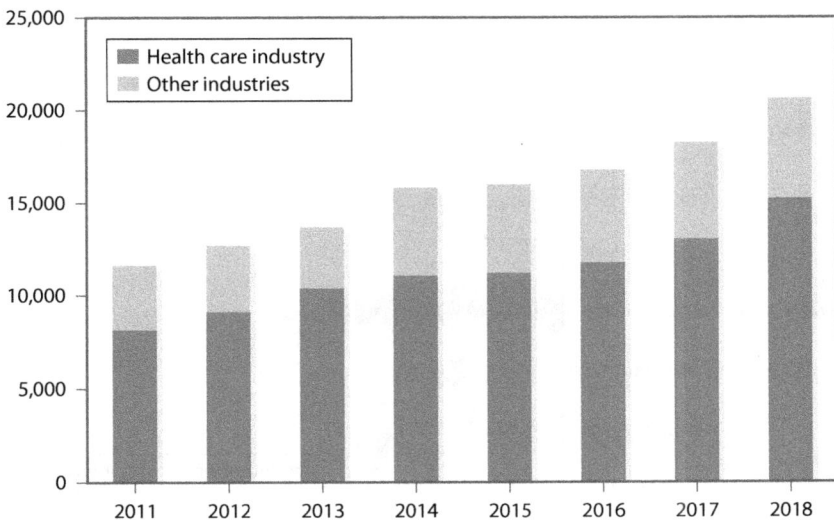

Figure 4.2: Number of Nonfatal WPV Injuries and Illnesses with Days Away from Work, 2011–2018 (6)

Table 4.3: Health care-Specific Incidence Rate (6)

Private Industry	NAICS code	Incidence rate of nonfatal intentional injury by other person, per 10,000 full-time workers
All Industry		2.1
Health care and social assistance	62	10.4
Ambulatory health care services	621	3.1
Hospitals	622	12.8
Psychiatric and substance abuse hospitals	6222	124.9
Nursing and residential care facilities	623	21.1
Social Assistance	624	12.4
Child day care services	6244	7.8

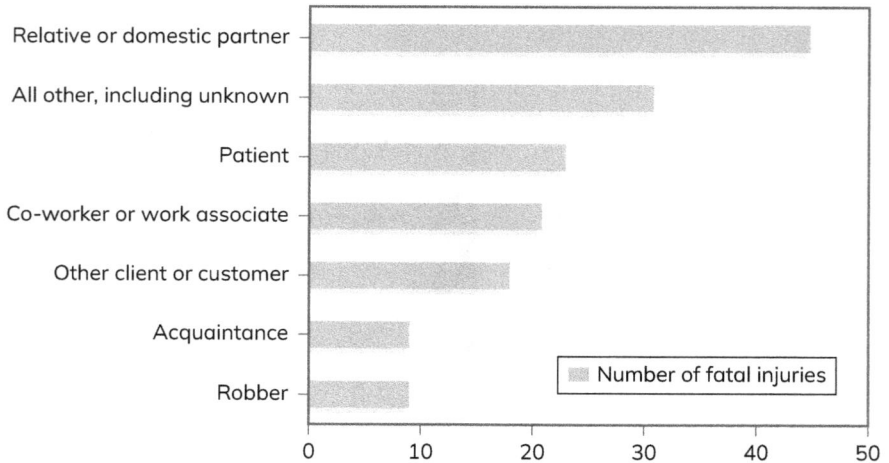

Figure 4.3: Workplace Homicides to Health care Workers in the United States by Assailant, 2011–2018 (6)

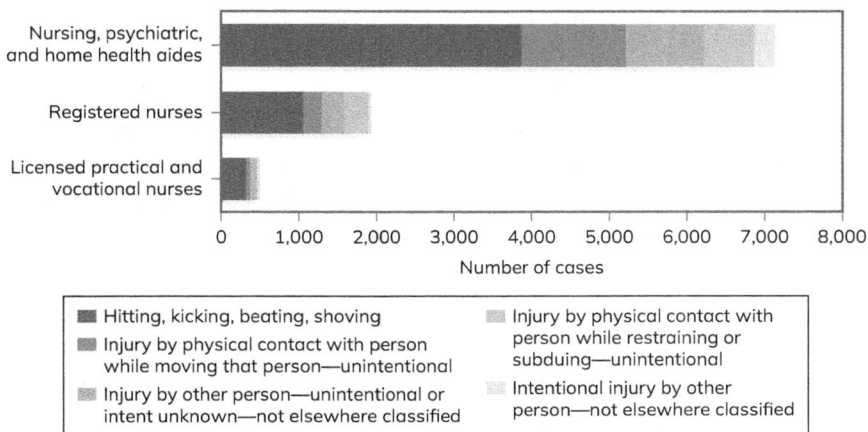

Figure 4.4: Violent Injuries Resulting in Days Away from Work, 2013 (7)

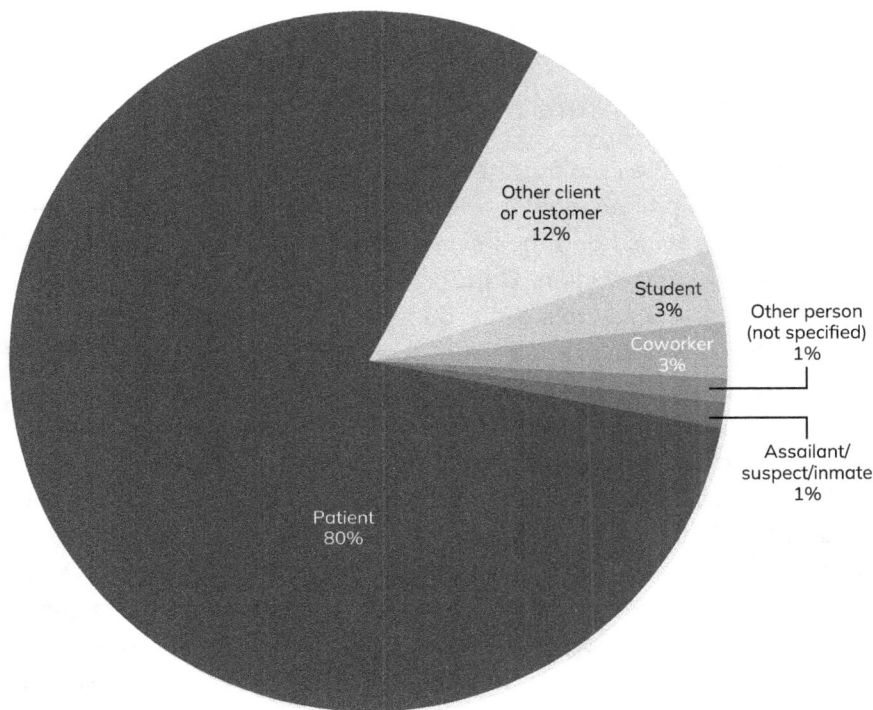

Figure 4.5: Health Care Worker Injuries Resulting in Days Away from Work by Source (7)

The Need to Collect Data

There is a legal requirement for employers to ensure a safe work environment. In order to achieve this goal, the employer has to assess the risks of the workplace. WPV is one of those risks. In Ontario, Canada, the provincial OHS Act, referred to as "the Act, Sec 30.0.3," puts a duty on the employer to assess the risk of WPV (2).

In the United States, the General Duty clause requires each employer to provide a workplace free from **hazards**. As of January 2022, all U.S. hospitals are required to conduct an annual WPV risk assessment (8). Risk assessments can be qualitative or quantitative. Qualitative assessments will require a person who is competent by means of knowledge and experience to conduct the assessment. For a quantitative analysis, one will need to collect data, analyze the data, and provide a mathematical interpretation. For the purposes of this chapter, focus will be on the quantitative data collection and analysis.

Statistics to Capture and Track

To assess a risk, the employer needs to collect data. Collection of quantitative data is predominantly a reactive function. Data here includes all incidents reported and their severity. Severity (S) of incidents is reviewed in the next section. Data collection provides a mathematical perspective of risk, enabling the quantification of data. Quantitative data lends to evaluation of potential predictive risks. The higher risk areas should be prioritized for interventions to reduce the risk of incidents.

Certain data points are considered necessary for appropriate incident tracking and trending. This data allows an organization to identify the highest risk locations and departments, the riskiest time of day, age groups, etc. This data should be gathered monthly and shared with important stakeholders. Total numbers of injuries should be visible to the WPV committee, executive leadership, and department directors/managers. Knowledge of this data helps point to where the risks are and helps set the priority for what training/education is needed. (Refer to Chapter 6 for more information on education based on risk.) Below are different types of WPV data points that can be collected to assess how to better manage WPV in an organization. A deeper analysis of incidents will pinpoint the areas, specific times, and type of events that caused WPV. Table 4.4 provides examples of the type of data to be collected, as a best practice.

Table 4.4: WPV Data Points

Date of Incident
Time of Incident
Building / Location of Incident
Department / Unit where Incident Occurred
Offender Name
Offender Type (Patient / Visitor / Student / Staff / Provider / etc.
Offender Gender
Offender Age
Summary of Event
Victim(s) Name
Victim Type (Patient / Visitor/ Student / Staff / Provider / etc.)
Victim Job Title (Nurse / Technician / Public Safety / Mental Health / Registration / Other, etc.)
Verbal Event (Yes / No)
Type of Verbal Event: <ul><li>Anxiety</li><li>Challenging / Untrusting</li><li>Refusal / Uncooperative</li><li>Yelling / Screaming</li><li>Threatening</li></ul>
Physical Contact (Yes / No)
Any injuries? (Yes / No)
Injury Data (Location of Injury, Mechanism of Injury)
Is it a reportable incident? (OSHA Reportable / Sentinel Event?)
Any lost work days/modified duty?

An incident may or may not result in injuries. Incidents range from **near-misses,** to injuries (I), and fatalities. Injury can be further classified as incident only, **medical aid** only, and medical aid with LT, depending on the outcome of the injury. **Near-miss** is technically a near-hit. This is an incident where the worker was not hurt but could have been hurt during the incident. A near-miss can also be referred to as a **hazard** in the workplace. Incidents and injuries are occurrences where the worker experiences an injury. **First Aid (FA)** is medical attention that is usually administered immediately after the injury occurs. If the FA was provided by a medical professional such as a registered nurse, it is then classified as a medical aid (MA). LT is anytime lost after an injury due to medical restrictions, treatments, or diagnosis. LT due to mental stress is now recognized as an occupational injury and being covered under the Workplace Safety and Insurance Board (WSIB). The WSIB is the province of Ontario, Canada's provincial body, that reimburses lost wages due to occupational injuries (9). Medical restriction refers to physical injury and mental stress. If a worker experiences an LT injury, but is able to return to work with limitations, it is considered **No Loss Time Medical Aid** (NLTMA). These are mainly Canadian definitions. The U.S. Bureau of Labor has other definitions for the same type on incidents. For example, LT for Canada is comparable to Days Away From Work and Days Away Restricted Time (DART) for NLTMA in the United States (10) (Table 4.5).

Table 4.5: Injury Classification

Canada	United States	Definition	Injury	Severity
Hazard	Hazard	Something with the potential to cause harm. Includes substances, equipment, machines, method of work, or the work environment		
Near-Miss	Near-Miss	Incident that did not cause any harm to the person		
Injury	Injury	Harm to an individual. Includes ill health and mental distress		
First Aid (FA)	First Aid (FA)	Harm to the person where one-time short treatment is administered by a first aider	May Be	
Medical Aid (MA)	Medical Aid (MA)	Harm to an individual that required treatment by a medical professional. Includes ill health and mental distress	Yes	
Loss Time (LT)	Lost Days Lost Time Injury (LTI)	Harm to an individual that required treatment by a medical professional and required time away from work for recovery. Includes ill health, mental distress, and permanent disability	Yes	Yes
No Loss Time Medical Aid (NLTMA)	Days Away Restricted Time (DART)	Days Away from work, days of restricted work activity, and/or days of jobs transfer	Yes	
Fatal	Fatal	Incident causing death	Yes	

Tracking an Injury Over Time

The two main categories used in the industry are Injury Rate (IR) and Severity Rate (SR). IR is the total number of injuries times 200,000 hours, divided by actual hours worked by all the current employees. The 200,000 hours represent the number of hours worked for 100 employees working a 40-hour work week and 50 weeks a year. SR is the total hours of LT multiplied by 200,000 hours, divided by # hours worked.

Injury Rate = Total Incidents × 200,000/Total Hours worked

Severity Rate = Total Hours Lost × 200,000/Total Hours Worked

Note that LT does not include the time lost on the day or the shift during which the incident occurred. LT is any subsequent time lost where the injured worker could not perform the regular scheduled work. Some employers will bring back the injured worker on modified duties based on the medical restrictions as prescribed by the treating physician, which is an NLTMA. Research has demonstrated that modified work improved the chances of return to preinjury duties (11).

Data Collection/Staff Reporting

A robust data collection process relies predominantly on establishing a successful reporting process in a culture that allows staff to feel informed and comfortable to report without retaliation. Every occurrence of WPV needs to be reported. WPV is often a behavior that is difficult to quantify since reporting relies on the victim to accurately document the behaviors or events that occurred. Because of that, accurate WPV statistics can be difficult to ascertain. Incident reports need to include the date and time, person affected, a factual description of what happened, any witness, severity of the injury if applicable, and measures taken to prevent reoccurrence. Severity here refers to the type of injury sustained and not the amount of time lost in the SR. Some organizations have information systems to manage such reports. Small and medium enterprises may not have the same resources and may be using a Word, Excel, or PDF fillable form or data manually tracked in an Excel file. Both have their advantages and disadvantages. To classify the incidents, an employer may make their own definitions; however, it is beneficial to utilize standardized definitions. It is highly recommended that organizations use the metrics as listed in the section "Statistics to Capture and Track."

Evaluating Potential Risk

Risk is a function of probability (P) and severity (S). Probability is the likelihood of the incident (12). Severity is the amount of harm that the incident will cause. To measure the probability of an incident, one must look at historical data and assess the frequency of incidents. For example, if historical data shows that there have been 10 incidents in a week, the probability measured in hours worked is 10/40, for a 40-hour workweek, resulting in a probability of 0.25*. The severity is a criterion that each employer can range from no injury/near-hit to critical injuries/death. The employer can quantify it as follows (Table 4.6):

Table 4.6: Example of Risk Rating Calculations

Severity Definition	Near-Hit	First Aid	Medical Aid	Medical Aid and Loss Time	Critical	Fatal
Severity range (S)	1	2	3	4	5	6
Probability (P)	0.25	0.25	0.25	0.25	0.25	0.25
Risk = S × P	0.25	0.5	0.75	1	1.25	1.5

Severity numbers can be rounded up to ensure that the risk rating is a whole number. In this example, the severity was rounded by a factor of 4, so the risks are quantified from 1 to 6 with 6 being the riskiest (Table 4.7).

Table 4.7: Risk Rating in Natural Number Range

Severity Definition	Near-Hit	First Aid	Medical Aid	Medical Aid and Loss Time	Critical	Fatal
Severity range (S)	4	8	12	16	20	24
Probability (P)	0.25	0.25	0.25	0.25	0.25	0.25
Risk = S × P	1	2	3	4	5	6

The organization can modify the probability criterion to fit their needs. For example, the probability can be measured as number of incidents

*The probability frequency formula used here is based on hours worked because it offers a true probability for the workplace being assessed. Many other authors simply define the probability as the likelihood of occurrence.

over the past month or quarter for tracking purposes. The severity range can even be increased, as displayed in Tables 4.8 and 4.9.

Probability for a monthly total of 10 incidents= $10/(40 \times 4) = 0.0625$ (See calculations in Table 4.8)

Table 4.8: Monthly Risk Rating Tracking

Severity Definition	Near-Hit	First Aid	Medical Aid	Medical Aid and Loss Time	Critical	Fatal
Severity range (S)	4	8	12	16	20	24
Probability (P)	0.02	0.02	0.02	0.02	0.02	0.02
Risk = S × P	0.25	0.5	0.75	1	1.25	1.5

Probability for a quarterly total of 10 incidents= $10/(40 \times 3 \times 4) = 0.16$ (See calculations in Table 4.9)

Table 4.9: Quarterly Risk Rating Tracking

Severity Definition	Near-Hit	First Aid	Medical Aid	Medical Aid and Loss Time	Critical	Fatal
Severity range (S)	4	8	12	16	20	24
Probability (P)	0.0208	0.0208	0.0208	0.0208	0.0208	0.0208
Risk = S × P	0.0833	0.1667	0.25	0.3333	0.4167	0.5

What to Do with the Data (Data Analysis)

The primary goal of data collection and analysis is to provide a mathematical view of the current state. Incident rates provide a rearview mirror on performance. The secondary goal is to prioritize WPV interventions to prevent recurrence. Interventions should follow the guidelines of any OHS program. Prevention programs can consist of formal or informal training, daily safety briefs, new standard work procedures to abide by, or even engineering physical changes to the workplace.

Prevention Controls

With detailed data tracking, one can determine which areas are experiencing high-volume and high-severity incidents. The next step is to identify the causes of the incidents and then apply mitigation strategies to prevent recurrence. Heinrich's "Inverse Pyramid for Control Measures" (Figure 4.6) suggests starting with eliminating the hazard (13). The idea behind this hierarchy is that the control methods at the top of the graphic are potentially more effective and protective than those at the bottom. Following this hierarchy normally leads to the implementation of inherently safer systems, where the risk of illness or injury has been substantially reduced (13).

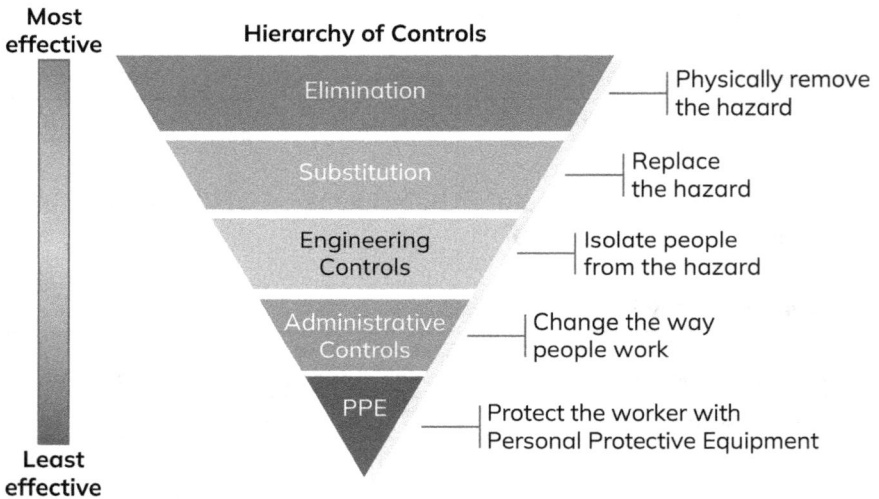

Most effective

Hierarchy of Controls

Elimination — Physically remove the hazard

Substitution — Replace the hazard

Engineering Controls — Isolate people from the hazard

Administrative Controls — Change the way people work

PPE — Protect the worker with Personal Protective Equipment

Least effective

Figure 4.6: Heinrich's Hierarchy of Controls

Each of the elements in Heinrich's inverse pyramid has to be assessed for feasibility and implementation. Elimination occurs when one can remove the hazard completely from the workplace or can build a process to completely prevent any hazards from occurring. In health care, WPV will always exist due to the nature of the operations because patients and caregivers are already under stress. This makes WPV difficult to fully eliminate. Substitution is working to prevent a known hazard by substituting it out. Substitution is not really an option for WPV either since human behavior cannot be predicted and people can be spontaneous and emotional, which creates no time to replace or plan for a different behavior. Therefore, elimination and substitution are not really feasible options. Engineering controls such as restricted access and physical barriers can reduce incidences of WPV by physically distancing the hazard or hazardous behaviors from the worker. Examples of this include restricted access areas, cameras that serve as deterrents, perimeter control to limit access, etc. Administrative controls consist of implementing measures to reduce the exposure to the hazards. In the context of WPV, examples of administrative controls include: WPV policies, reporting processes, de-escalation training, partnership agreements, and reducing the number of visitors or caregivers allowed for a patient. One of the main administrative measures is training for employees. Training should focus on what type of WPV or risk the workers are subjected to and how the workers can improve their ability to manage such situations, in efforts to control and prevent WPV incidents from occurring. Personal protective equipment (PPE) is the last resort of prevention measures. Health care workers already wear a host of PPE to prevent exposure to biological and chemical hazards. In the context of **Workplace Violence Prevention (WPVP)**, PPE can be Kevlar sleeves to prevent bites and scratches, padded vests and gloves when working with known violent patients. Other PPEs include eye protection, face shields, Kevlar vests and hoodies, or even a helmet in extreme cases.

Since we cannot completely eliminate WPV at work, we can start by improving the work culture to be safer. Safety culture is how the workplace is perceived by the worker. This perception influences the engagement level of the worker to identify, assess, and correct hazards. Recent studies have demonstrated that OHS training combined with an interactive means of **communication** has a positive effect on perception of safety culture (14). A positive workplace culture can also improve patient care (15). Health care costs such as sick time, absenteeism, and medical costs can improve with an improved workplace safety culture as well (16).

Communicating Potential Risks

Communication about risk awareness can be one of the main prevention methods. Communication can take many forms. Digital communication is the main platform the industry uses. These digital communications are e-mails, computer-based learning modules through a Learning Management System (LMS), or even phone/electronic documentation and message alerts. Verbal communications should purposefully occur during meetings and briefings. Communication is the coding of a message and transfer to the intended recipient. However, for effective communication, the recipient needs to be able to decode the message and receive the intended message. **Effective communication** is "the ability to convey facts, concepts, or reasoning clearly to others, and to receive and understand the messages sent by others" (17). We must be aware that the recipients will have their own prior information, experiences, and biases that will affect reception of the message. Therefore, when communicating risks to the workforce, the employer has to implement effective communication channels.

Continuous Quality Improvement

Continuous Quality Improvement (CQI) is a quality management process that looks at processes, procedures, and outcomes, with the intent to enhance and better operations. CQI is synonymous with the Plan–Do–Study–Act (PDSA) cycle of improvement (18). Many organizations offer PDSA training and some offer more detailed quality/continuous improvement training. Based on the data and information discussed in the previous paragraphs, one can appreciate which direction to take for improvement. Another method is to institute a culture of ownership among staff. Ownership here refers to be accountable for safety at their level. This helps foster the internal responsibility system as well as a culture where people identify risks/concerns and actively act/move forward on mitigating the risk. The workplace culture is influenced by many factors that staff are exposed to. Internal factors are the training and directions provided by the employer, leadership, and peers. External factors are communications from broader social media. Large-scale interventions are required to influence workers toward a culture of ownership. These interventions can be training the employee on hazards assessment and implementing control measures within their own units. This can prevent incidents from escalating to a physical altercation that results in injury (19). The data (injury/incident rates along with other key metrics) will provide an indication whether the organization is moving in the right direction, that is, a decreasing IR over time. CQI can be leveraged in areas with the highest risks. Reviewing data/metrics in a transparent manner with the entire team allows management to foster a problem-solving, solution-focused culture and encourages team members to implement/maintain the controls that organizations put in place to mitigate risk. Leveraging CQI allows organizations to evaluate risk, implement improvement opportunities, and track appropriate metrics to confirm positive change.

An organization can choose from several metrics to measure workplace risks. Metrics have the ability to provide a numerical perspective on the performance of the organization. The parameters to measure the performance should be relevant to identifying WPV risk. Prioritizing the highest risks helps in reducing WPV incidents. A reduction in such incidents improves workplace culture, staff engagement, and patient care. The health care sector is experiencing higher demands from the public. A positive workplace safety culture can meet those demands effectively.

References

1. d'Ettorre, Gabriele, and Vincenza Pellicani. 2017. "Workplace Violence Toward Mental Healthcare Workers Employed in Psychiatric Wards." *Safety and Health at Work* 8 (4): 337–342.
2. Ontario. n.d. "Occupational Health and Safety Act." *Ontario Laws.* Accessed February 8, 2022. https://www.ontario.ca/laws/statute/90o01#BK60.
3. AWCBC. n.d. "2019 Lost Time Claims in Canada." Accessed March 1, 2022. https://awcbc.org/en/statistics/.
4. USBL. n.d. "Survey of Occupational Injuries and Illnesses Data." *Injuries, Illnesses, and Fatalities.* Accessed March 1, 2022. https://www.bls.gov/iif/soii-data.htm.
5. Yassi, Annalee, and Tina Hancock. 2005. "Patient Safety—Worker Safety: Building a Culture of Safety to Improve Healthcare Worker and Patient Well-Being." *Healthcare Quarterly* Oct: 32–38.
6. BLS. n.d. *Fact Sheet | Workplace Violence in Healthcare, 2018 | April 2020.* Accessed March 23, 2022. https://www.bls.gov/iif/oshwc/cfoi/workplace-violence-healthcare-2018.htm.
7. OSHA. n.d. "Workplace Violence in Healthcare." Accessed March 22, 2022. https://www.dedicatednurses.com/wp-content/uploads/2020/01/4.2019-Workplace-Violence-in-Healthcare.pdf.
8. Joint Commission. 2021. "Workplace Violence Prevention Standards." June 18. http://www.jointcommission.org/-/media/tjc/documents/standards/r3-reports/wpvp-r3_20210618.pdf.

9.   WSIB. 2022. "Work-Related Mental Stress Injuries." March 17. Accessed March 17, 2022. https://www.wsib.ca/en/injured-or-ill-people/claims/work-related-mental-stress-injuries.

10. USBLS. n.d. "Fatal Occupational Injuries for Selected Occupations, 2016-20." Accessed March 1, 2022. https://www.bls.gov/news.release/cfoi.t03.htm.

11. Yassi, A., R. Tate, A. J. Cooper, C. Snow, S. Vallentyne, and J. B. Khokar. 1995. "Early Intervention for Back-Injured Nurses at a Large Canadian Tertiary Care Hospital: An Evaluation of the Effectiveness and Cost Benefits of a Two-Year Pilot Project." *Occupational Medicine* 45 (4). Accessed March 5, 2022. https://doi.org/10.1093/occmed/45.4.209.

12. ACS Institute. n.d. "Risk Rating & Assessment." Accessed March 14, 2022. https://institute.acs.org/lab-safety/hazard-assessment/fundamentals/risk-assessment.html.

13. NIOSH. n.d. "Hierarchy of Controls." Accessed February 14, 2022. https://www.cdc.gov/niosh/topics/hierarchy/default.html.

14. Ahadzi, Dzifa Francis, Abdul-Rahaman Afitiri, and Elizabeth Ahadzi. 2021. "Organizational Safety Culture Perceptions of Healthcare Workers in Ghana: A Cross-Sectional Interview Study." *International Journal of Nursing Studies Advances* 3: 100020.

15. Brathwaite, Jeffrey, Jessica Herkes, Kristiana Ludlow, Testa Luke, and Gina Lamprell. 2017. "Association between Organisational and Workplace Cultures, and Patient Outcomes: Systematic Review." *BMJ Open* 7: e017708. doi: 10.1136/bmjopen-2017-017708.

16. Fabius, Raymond, Sharon Glave Frazee, Dixon Thayer, David Kirshenbaum, and Jim Reynold. 2018. "The Correlation of a Corporate Culture of Health Assessment Score and Health Care Cost Trend." *Journal of Occupational Medicine* 60 (6): 507–514.

17. Dyck, Dianne E. G. 2015. *Occupational Health and Safety.* Markham, ON: Lexis Nexis.

18. ASQ. n.d. "What Is the Plan-Do-Check-Act (PDCA) Cycle?" Accessed February 15, 2022. https://asq.org/quality-resources/pdca-cycle.

19. Van Scheppingen, Arjella R., Ernest M.M. de Vroome, Kristin C. J. M. ten Have, Ellen H. Bos, Gerard I. J. M Zwetsloot, and W. van Mechelen. 2014. "Inducing a Health-Promoting Change Process within an Organization." *Journal of Occupational and Environmental Medicine* 56 (11): 1128–1136.

Glossary of Terms

Communication The ability to convey facts, concepts, or reasoning clearly to others, and to receive and understand the messages sent by others.

Continuous Quality Improvement (CQI) A quality management process that looks at processes, procedures, and outcomes with the intent to enhance and better operations.

First Aid (FA) An injury where treatment was administered by a qualified first aider or self-administered. The injury did not require medical treatment by a professional medical practitioner.

Hazard An object or process which may cause an injury. The object can be chemical, physical, biological and the process can be psychosocial.

Injury (I) A person being hurt by physical, chemical, biological, or psychosocial agents. The harm can be medical or mental.

Lost Time (LT) An injury serious enough to warrant a health care provider to restrict an employee from their regular job duties for a specified period of time. The injured cannot resume the next scheduled full-duty shift. The day of the injury is not considered Lost Time.

Medical Aid (MA) An injury where the person requires medical treatment provided by a professional medical practitioner. Medical Aid includes first aid administered by a professional medical practitioner.

Medical Aid No Lost Time An injury where the victim requires medical attention/aid and is able to resume work, but with medical restrictions. May also be called Modified Duty or Light Duty.

Near-Miss An event where a person was not injured but came close to being injured.

Workplace Harassment (Ontario Definition)
   a. Engaging in a course of vexatious comment or conduct against a worker in a workplace that is known or ought reasonably to be known to be unwelcome, or
   b. Workplace sexual harassment;

Workplace Sexual Harassment (Ontario Definition)
a.   Engaging in a course of vexatious comment or conduct against a worker in a workplace because of sex, sexual orientation, gender identity, or gender expression, where the course of comment or conduct is known or ought reasonably to be known to be unwelcome, or
b.   Making a sexual solicitation or advance where the person making the solicitation or advance is in a position to confer, grant, or deny a benefit or advancement to the worker and the person knows or ought reasonably to know that the solicitation or advance is unwelcome;

Workplace Violence (WPV) (Ontario Definition)
a.   The exercise of physical force by a person against a worker, in a workplace, that causes or could cause physical injury to the worker,
b.   An attempt to exercise physical force against a worker, in a workplace, that could cause physical injury to the worker,
c.   A statement or behavior that is reasonable for a worker to interpret as a threat to exercise physical force against the worker, in a workplace, that could cause physical injury to the worker.

Workplace Violence (WPV)—U.S. Definition Any act or threat of physical violence, harassment, intimidation, or other threatening disruptive behavior that occurs at the work site.

Workplace Violence Prevention (WPVP) A system of attitudes, strategies, practices, initiatives, and behaviors that work to stop and prevent any acts of threat, harassment, intimidation, or disruptive behavior from occurring at a place of employment.

CHAPTER 5

Executive Ownership: Leading from the Front

Deb Somers-Larney

CPI

Objectives

After reading this chapter, one should be able to:

- Understand how responsibility for workplace violence prevention rests on the shoulders of the chief executive officer and appointed senior executives
- Identify why leadership needs a multidepartmental approach to support workplace violence prevention strategies
- Incrementally establish a program, regardless of initial budget
- Recognize the superpowers of middle managers as "force multipliers" in the workplace violence prevention program
- Identify how to get buy-in and drive workforce engagement
- Understand the concerns about zero-tolerance language

In the United States, the Occupational Safety and Health Act of 1970 (OSH Act) includes a "General Duty Clause" that requires employers to provide a workplace "free from recognized hazards that are causing or likely to cause death or serious physical harm" and may not retaliate against those who report concerns (1). The **Occupational Safety and Health Administration (OSHA)** provides an excellent and comprehensive resource for establishing a compliant **workplace violence prevention (WPVP)** program in its "Guidelines for Preventing Workplace Violence for Health Care and Social Service Workers." Similarly, **Canada's Centre for Occupational Health and Safety (CCOHS)** Acts legally require organizations to incorporate WPVP practices to protect worker safety. So, if these guidelines give a road map that is equally useful in all organizations and countries, why is this handbook still necessary?

Comprehensive WPVP programs have not been the norm. By and large, health care organizations focused on **patient safety** and treated **workplace violence (WPV)** as a security problem for **Public Safety** departments to solve. They also tended to focus on public safety response to violent incidents specifically in hospitals. But the understanding of WPVP is evolving, and employees rightly demand reforms that commit to the safety and health of employees, not just patients. Further, they seek recognition that employees may be in hospitals, clinics, office buildings, or even in the patient's home, and they deserve to be safe everywhere. In addition, WPVP requirements are also now appropriately integrated into health care accreditation systems. Clearly, organizations must step up or face sanctions, alienate employees, or, worse, allow significant risks to go unchecked. WPVP is a daunting prospect—so how does an organization proceed in building a program that will work?

CEO and Senior Executive Responsibilities

The **Chief Executive Officer (CEO)** is responsible for WPVP and should ensure that the Board of Directors is regularly updated on progress. The CEO should assign accountability to a senior executive with sufficient scope of responsibility and authority in the system's governance model. For example, the Chief Nursing Officer, Chief Human Resources Officer, etc., are appropriate choices. Regrettably, the senior public safety leader is usually not afforded that level of organizational responsibility. So, while the public safety leader will be a critical part of the program, they are probably not the right choice to lead it alone. Employees, patients, or visitors could be violent anywhere, whether in hospitals, clinic, or offices, so the WPVP program must be organization-wide, and will require multidisciplinary cooperation. To comply with governmental, accreditation, and other regulations, WPVP efforts must be woven into all normal operations, training, and standard recordkeeping. In this respect, it is comparable to the patient safety journey, wherein all employees are educated, all incidents are reported, the most severe incidents undergo a swift cause analysis, and concrete remediations are assigned to an accountable party(ies). The WPVP program executive sponsor must have the authority to assign WPVP goals and objectives to all types of leaders across the system and to harness organizational resources in support of the program. At the highest level, the senior executive sponsor should convene a standing workgroup or committee of supporting department executives, for example, medical and nursing staff governance, human resources, training, legal, compliance, public safety, construction, facilities maintenance, patient safety, emergency department governance, and public affairs. Specifically, include a representative who can address challenges in including nonemployee physicians and providers, both for training and compliance. This group would form the overall organizational WPVP committee. Each of the subordinate entities should mirror the organization's committee with their own committee, to implement the program at the local level (e.g., in each hospital, for regional or ambulatory sites, etc. For more information on committees in the Ambulatory or Alternate sites, refer to Chapter 9.)

"Give Me a Metaphor ..."

Resources like the OSHA guidelines may provide a road map for WPVP definitions and processes, but that is not sufficient to garner the cooperation that is needed to make an effective program. The organization, through the senior executive sponsor and a supporting executive committee, should strive to create an integrated protection strategy through policies, standard procedures, everyday practices, and culture. Metaphorically imagine the WPVP program to be a shield made of overlapping protective armored plates, or a safety umbrella with supporting ribs. Whatever the metaphor, use it to communicate a unifying strategy that conveys the expectation that all will collectively contribute to and benefit from WPVP.

Create a culture that is kind, consistent, calm, and fair. This must be the baseline expectation of employees, patients, and visitors in every facility, so that anything contrary is easily identified. The executive sponsor can champion the cause and demonstrate to employees that the system is equally committed to *their* safety. A charismatic executive leader with the authority to bring the full force of the system to bear on the issue can be an engagement triumph. Done well, this leadership will ensure success while bolstering a culture of ownership, empowerment, and cooperation.

"How to Begin?"

The executive sponsor should lead the executive staff to first use what probably already exists. The organization already has processes for managing *patient safety* risks with goals and objectives and regular reassessment. The organization has intelligent employees who are organized in definable work units. They are accustomed to reporting detailed facts and complying with quality improvement processes. Tuck WPVP under the larger patient safety process and begin to track it the same way.

Treat workplace safety as a personal obligation in which all employees engage, as opposed to something public safety provides *for* them. Harness employee pride and altruism into a sense of fierce team-centered protectiveness. If the WPVP executive committee can create a culture where employees are engaged as a team to protect their home turf and each other, you have effectively multiplied the number of eyes and ears trained and dedicated to preserving safety. To foster engagement, invite employees and providers to provide in-put. Town Hall meetings, surveys, **rounding** initiatives, and voluntary workgroups are ways to invite employees to explain their challenges. Only the executive team has the authority and resources to be able to institute that kind of campaign.

Leadership Support for a Multidepartmental Approach

"Do We Need Hand-to-Hand Combat Training?"

WPVP does not expect employees to physically intervene to prevent violence. Rather, mutually supporting standards and de-escalation strategies, when used together, will make a positive impact. It may be helpful to broadly envision WPVP activities in terms of three key components: PREPARE, PROTECT, and REACT. We should PREPARE patients, employees, providers, and visitors to succeed; use a variety of strategies to PROTECT them from lasting harm; and REACT appropriately when violence occurs and in response to near misses. Examples of common key strategies follow:

WPVP Strategies

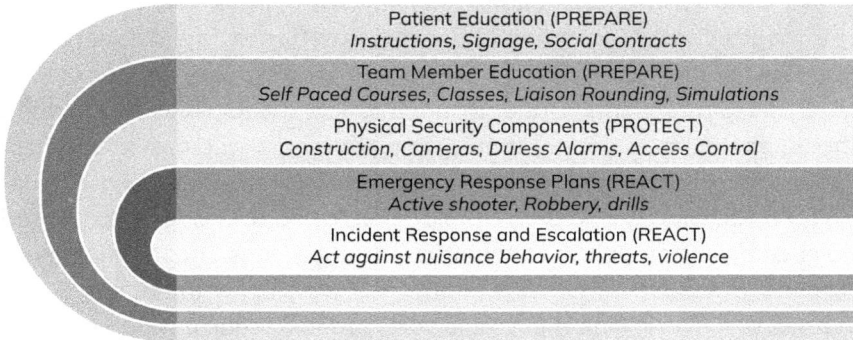

Patient Education (PREPARE)
Instructions, Signage, Social Contracts

Team Member Education (PREPARE)
Self Paced Courses, Classes, Liaison Rounding, Simulations

Physical Security Components (PROTECT)
Construction, Cameras, Duress Alarms, Access Control

Emergency Response Plans (REACT)
Active shooter, Robbery, drills

Incident Response and Escalation (REACT)
Act against nuisance behavior, threats, violence

Strategy	Example of Key Activities
Patient Education (PREPARE)	Signs that establish expectations, language in patients' rights documents, social contracts in response to first-time or low-level offenses; employees communicate and enforce clear and consistent norms to patients and visitors, threat assessments
Employee/Provider Education (PREPARE)	Basic WPV awareness and reporting education for 100% of employees and physicians, integrate WPV incident data into the broader safety reporting process, brainstorm the most common threatening situations at the work unit level and discuss, add violence prevention in nursing simulations, leader rounding, public safety rounding, threat assessments
Physical Environment (PROTECT)	Physical design that supports security, security cameras and recording, access control, panic buttons, ensure daily operations correctly use the environment and security features, choose security over convenience, threat assessments
Response Plans and Practice (REACT)	Work unit level practice of common scenarios, robbery drills, active shooter drills, evacuation plans, crisis communication drills, use plain language, threat assessments
Incident Response, Escalation, and Remediation (REACT)	De-escalation of threatening behavior, call for help, facilitate first responders, evacuate, post evacuation reconstitution, incident reporting, conduct incident analysis, ensure remediation, provide victim assistance, ongoing threat assessments

The breadth of these strategies demonstrates that many different departments support the overall WPVP program. Only system executive leaders have the authority to weave WPVP into the fabric of the system and maintain oversight over performance in this way. For example, executive leaders should ensure threat assessments occur at every stage to enable continuous improvement of the committees. The construction department and public safety should establish physical security standards; Public Safety provides security infrastructure, severe incident response, and documentation; the facilities department should implement signage, lighting improvements, and regular maintenance; the training department should develop role-appropriate training for all employees, nursing simulations should be modified to include violence de-escalation scenarios; non-hospital sites should implement practical exercises in the work area; the safety department should integrate WPV incidents into the broader safety reporting process and train employees on how to report; the information technology department might implement communications with home health providers so they can communicate from the field, etc. This is a terrific opportunity for the CEO and staff to demonstrate their commitment and make lasting improvements.

Budgeting for WPV

Reviewing the example WPVP strategies discussed earlier, the system executive may need to initially implement the program using existing resources. Many strategies apply existing safety methodology in novel ways, adding new goals and objectives, and new processes with minimal direct cost.

- Organizational, departmental, and personal accountabilities for personal conduct as well as incident reporting
- Risk analyses for processes and work areas; consensus on risk tolerance (e.g., how to respond to nuisance behavior that does not cause serious harm)
- Appropriate staffing and scheduling practices to ensure that staff are not made vulnerable
- Concise policies

- Organizational policy education, role-based training, simulations, and practical exercises for the most likely scenarios in
  each type of work site
- An easy, effective, and reliable incident reporting process, perhaps that expands upon an existing patient safety incident reporting process.

Future budgetary needs will become clearer as the organization
works through the risk assessment process (refer to the OSHA guidelines). For example, risks stemming from a lack of physical security
standards will underscore the need for committed capital funding and
the assessments will target the highest priority items first.

Initially, training will at least require budget for lost work hours for all
employees (with higher risk employees receiving more training). Some organizations can use internal training resources while others may opt for a
vendor-provided program. Regardless, the WPVP training series should
be tiered, based on employee work responsibilities. It must include baseline training for all employees about WPVP expectations, rights, norms,
and reporting. All employees should understand what constitutes unacceptable behavior and should follow a consistent approach for de-escalation. Employees must also practice as a work unit to know when to
disengage and escalate the challenging situation to their leaders and/or
Public Safety team. Also, it can be prohibitively expensive and challenging to set aside time for dedicated training. Consider supplemental micro
training. For example, use more frequent quick video refreshers (think
TikTok) and scenarios that apply to the actual work environment. Strive
to provide very targeted content that reinforces de-escalation techniques
and is short enough to include at shift change briefings or unit meetings.
(For more information on training, refer to Chapter 6.)

Capturing incident data may prove a difficult challenge. Some
organizations may have to compile statistics manually in an iterative
process while others have web-based incident reporting. Purchasing or
modifying the incident reporting capability is a common cost that can
provide excellent **Return on Investment (ROI)** from a risk avoidance and
employee engagement perspective. Regardless of the reporting process,
ensure that serious violence is escalated up to the responsible executive
and WPVP committee. Statistics will inform whether training is appropriate, and which work units and sites need help. Remember, different

levels of government may impose WPVP responsibilities, so ensure that all the sites in the organization have clarity on their regulations.

Middle Management as Superpowers

Middle managers are an underutilized force multiplier in the WPVP program. This population holds much information that is critical to the risk analysis process. They are intimately familiar with the work area and the specific types of threats their unit encounters. A fundamental crime prevention principle recognizes that employees provide the greatest threat information because they are most familiar with their work area. They know what is routine and can spot the unusual. Managers can sensitize their team to quickly identify and report on anomalies. Cultivate specific messaging and encouragement for this important group. Not everyone has a public safety responder available to them, but everyone does have a manager, so leveraging them makes sense. Middle managers should:

- Provide key insight about an offending employee. If an employee is a risk or has acted violently, their manager should serve on the activated incident **Threat Assessment Team**. The manager may provide insight into mindset, work history, resilience, behavior, and personal life.
- Maintain enough genuine familiarity with their team members to understand whether they are at risk of domestic violence spilling into the work setting. Urge at-risk employees to report the domestic violence concerns to public safety. Public safety should collaborate with the manager to create a personal safety plan. For example, a stalking victim may be moved to temporarily work in a different department and park in a different area.
- Build team confidence. Lead the work unit in situational mini exercises right in the work area, practicing their most common challenging situations. Practice the most common interactions, like de-escalating an uncooperative patient. Practice how co-workers should use each other to manage a situation. Lead the work unit in practicing crisis evacuation procedures (e.g., fire and active shooter use the same escape routes).
- Advocate for their team. Escalate questions. Make provisions for staff to be freed up to attend trainings. Provide feedback

about whether training, incident collection processes, or policies are clear or burdensome.

- Allay employee fears. Support honest incident reporting, as employees are fearful of retribution or of being blamed for an incident.
- Put the employee first. Provide daily leadership rounding and safe scheduling, for example, to ensure that employees are not scheduled to work alone in a remote location.
- Reinforce the team approach. Serve as the calming "adult" to counter fear and reinforce training principles in their specific work area. Cultivate a "work family" that protects each other with proactive verbal de-escalation as a team.
- Ensure accuracy. The incident reporting process can be weaponized, causing unintended consequences. Employees may use the process to register grudges. Staff may inflate language in incident reports to justify getting more staff or some other improvement. While all reports must be investigated, a critical eye is necessary.
- Take primary responsibility for victim assistance if an incident does occur. Ensure the employee and any impacted coworkers receive appropriate encouragement, mental health, and physical support.
- CELEBRATE SUCCESS. When a work unit correctly applies their de-escalation training, publicly celebrate them. Use their stories to promote best practices.

Workforce Engagement: How to Get Buy-In

Due to legal obligations and regulations, organizations are required to develop prevention strategies, but may not yet have funding. So how does an organization move forward with this? As described earlier, creating the WPVP program is a straightforward process. A great deal can be accomplished before funding is needed. But it will not succeed without incident reporting. Obviously, public safety reports are a logical start. But public safety officers only report on the incidents to which they were summoned. Many more incidents occur that do not require public safety, or in an area with no public safety resources. How can leadership get buy-in from all employees?

First, the sponsoring executive leader should assign the public relations/marketing department to create an internal campaign in support of the WPV program. The campaign should be rolled out in conjunction with training content that explains personal responsibilities of WPVP. Consider piggybacking the WPVP messaging in other existing communications and newsletters with a slogan or metaphor that promotes a feeling of empowerment.

Simplify reporting to gain maximum compliance. As reporting of patient safety and violent incidences is burdensome, it is important to streamline the inputs to the process. It is equally important for site WPVP committees to read the input, prioritize incidents, laud excellent de-escalation, encourage employees, and respond. Employees will expect a reply or may want to know the outcome of follow-up, although the volume of low-level nuisance incidents will make that difficult. After reviewing the incident, consider using a standard reply for low-risk incidents that thanks the employee for reporting and informs them that the situation has been reviewed, and that no further action is warranted at this time. A link or process to appeal can also be included in the response to the employee, in the event that they want to appeal that determination. Significant incidents should be quickly escalated to the overall organizational committee for further review and follow-up.

Employees will be more likely to report incidents if they receive/ see the benefit of their reporting. Provide metrics to demonstrate effectiveness of the effort. Celebrate excellent de-escalation responses. Use those "wins" for future communications.

Next, use what already exists. Get in front of the various employee and governance councils to alert them to the WPVP program. Highlight the fact that the system is demonstrating commitment to employee safety. Provide multiple ways in which employees can send questions or suggestions. To further reinforce the critical role of the middle manager, have the comments and suggestions go through their manager. Ask the managers to consolidate/clarify the issues before sending them to the WPVP committee.

Build metrics into the WPVP program and push those metrics out to demonstrate effectiveness of the effort. Publish reporting goals the same as would occur for patient safety reporting. Track them as key performance indicators and publish the results.

Note that even though WPVP incident reporting will ultimately help employees, it is "one more thing" that busy people are being asked to do. Cultivate buy-in from middle managers. They may see the WPVP program as irrelevant. Impaired patients will continue to threaten and lash out, but now employees are asked to tally it all. Explain how the program will help caregivers recognize problems early on, attempt de-escalation, position themselves correctly to minimize harm, and practice a team approach to the incident. Be prepared to have to explain that even though low-level aggression is probably inevitable, employees should be safer. Focus on superb reporting and response for severe incidents, as opposed to worrying over the thousands of minor nuisance incidents.

The "Z Word"—Concerns about Zero tolerance Language

To demonstrate their commitment, some organizations employ the phrase "zero tolerance" in their WPVP policies. They may have posted signs advising patients that the facility has zero tolerance of violence and that violators will be referred to police, or that employees who violate the zero-tolerance policy will be terminated. What does zero tolerance mean? This is an important question. If the organization chooses to use "zero tolerance" language in its signage and policies, it will almost certainly cause some confusion and must be carefully defined. Even if we use the term "zero tolerance," certainly, some violence will still be tolerated. For example, a threat technically constitutes violence, and patients in crisis will continue to shout out threats. A patient who pushes a nurse's hand away also commits violence. Yet, there is no meaningful way in which that act will "not be tolerated." The patient will not be dismissed. Charges will not be pressed. So, what does zero tolerance mean?

> In a clinic, a doctor was suddenly and viciously attacked by a patient. As the victim's coworkers struggled to pull the patient off the doctor, they felt helpless, as they were afraid to harm the attacker. They would not use force of any kind to strike the attacker because they were afraid to get fired due to the zero-tolerance policy. The victim was afraid to utilize the items in his pocket (scissors, pens, etc.) to strike back to get free. Their misinterpretation of zero tolerance only came to light during the incident debrief with the site manager. This led to an important clarification in the policy as well as in training.

The goal of the WPVP program is to identify workplace hazards and seek to eliminate or control them to prevent serious injury from violence. Instead of "zero tolerance," consider language that instead states the expectation of a violence-free environment and *reserves* the right to act. Similarly, be careful with language in the employee policy. A "zero-tolerance" policy might be weaponized to terminate an unpopular employee for making a threat or touching a coworker on the shoulder. But if another employee is not terminated for similar actions, the organization may be at risk for a discrimination suit. Further, there may be times when violence is warranted, such as to intervene in an attack. Standard active shooter response directs, "Run, Hide, Fight." The obvious implication is that the situation (being under attack) justifies any action, including violence. Better to carefully phrase the policy to clarify defensive versus offensive actions.

A mature WPVP program is comprehensive, with components woven into every aspect of the organization. Incremental progress is possible with meaningful senior executive leadership that assigns goals and objectives and ensures accountability. The WPVP program should be a source of great pride and accomplishment, as it represents the whole of the organization taking positive control of its environment and demanding safety for its workers.

Reference

1. OSHA 3148-06R 2016. *Guidelines for Preventing Workplace Violence for Healthcare and Social Service Workers*. U.S. Department of Labor Occupational Safety and Health Administration.

Glossary of Terms

Canadian Centre for Occupational Health and Safety (CCOHS) An independent departmental corporation under the Financial Administration Act that is accountable to Parliament through the Ministry of Labour that functions as the primary national agency in Canada for the advancement of safe and healthy workplaces by preventing work-related injuries, illnesses, and deaths, by providing information, training, education, and management systems and solutions.

Chief Executive Officer (CEO) The senior-most executive of the health care entity, be it a system or an independent hospital.

Occupational Safety and Health Administration (OSHA) A large regulatory agency of the U.S. Federal Department of Labor that ensures safe and healthful working conditions for workers by setting and enforcing standards and by providing training, outreach, education, and assistance.

Patient Safety Comprehensive programs in which health care organizations methodically track and reduce harm to patients (e.g., hospital-acquired infections, medical treatment errors, etc.) by counting harmful incidents, performing cause analyses, and implementing continual improvements to reduce future incidents.

Public Safety A department in a health care system that has a broad span of responsibilities, some of which include managing safety and security incidents, responding to emergency incidents, de-escalating verbal and physical disturbances, assisting with keeping patients safe, handling access control and identification of staff, and managing parking responsibilities. Sometimes referred to as the "Security" or "Protection" department.

Return on Investment (ROI) A performance measure used to evaluate the efficiency or profitability of a program. ROI measures the program value or benefits, relative to the investment costs.

Rounding Walking through workplace departments to regularly check in with employees (similar to medical staff making patient rounds). It can be used to assess morale, demonstrate engagement, confirm compliance, etc.

Threat Assessment Team A team or committee that convenes to assess a WPV incident or threat to coordinate an organizational response in a unified and efficient way. (For example, if a patient threatens a nurse, the team will decide if the threat is significant and how best to counter it. They will gather facts like the patient's medical and mental diagnoses, current stressors, ability to cause harm, weapon ownership, circumstances that triggered the threat, and whether they have previous incidents, to decide an appropriate response.)

Workplace Violence (WPV) Any act or threat of physical violence, harassment, intimidation, or other threatening disruptive behavior that occurs at the work site.

Workplace Violence Prevention (WPVP) A system of attitudes, strategies, practices, initiatives, and behaviors that work to stop and prevent any acts of threat, harassment, intimidation, or disruptive behavior from occurring at a place of employment.

CHAPTER 6

Managing Training and Education Needs

Kimberly A. Urbanek

CPI

Objectives

After reading this chapter, one should be able to:

- Identify five training program challenges in health care
- Understand four types of violence and how they shape training curriculum
- Understand how to assign a risk level to specific areas of the organization
- Create an education plan for each risk level
- Identify various types of training opportunities

Developing a robust training program for **workplace violence prevention (WPVP)** is really the only way to make organizational policies, procedures, and philosophies come to life in a successful way. However, there are many layers to this and many ways to tackle how to provide training for a prevention program. This chapter will explore ideas of who to train, types of training needed, and how to determine risk levels so that appropriate training can be developed and delivered for each level.

Health Care Training Challenges

The health care industry presents many unique challenges when it comes to providing **workplace violence (WPV)** training across the organization. It is best to have a tiered and diversified approach to be able to conquer the distinctly different areas that exist in health care. Therefore, it is critical to first understand what not to do when designing training, so that the prevention program will be beneficial to everyone completing it. Below are five pitfalls that outline what **not to do** when designing your training program.

Health Care Training Pitfalls

1. "One Size Fits All" Approach
   The health care industry is a vastly diverse world with a lot of moving parts. Therefore, no one training approach will cover all entities. Many nuisances need to be considered when developing training platforms for your organization. Training will need to look different, depending on the target audience. Assigning a single lesson to everyone in the organization is not a successful way to build a culture of violence prevention since training will need to be tailored to individual areas. Creating some differentiation in your training will make it more efficient and applicable to the differing areas that exist.

   Solution: Create a variety of training options tailored to fit the specific needs of the staff.

   The factors below should be considered when deciding how to design a training program that incorporates all aspects of the organization:

   Training considerations:
   - In-hospital setting versus ambulatory settings
   - Clinical roles versus non-clinical roles
   - Employed roles versus non-employed roles (providers/physicians/volunteers, etc.)
   - Frontline staff versus management staff
   - Full-time staff versus registry (PRN) staff
   - 24/7/365 departments versus daily business operations

2. "Checking the Boxes" Approach
   It is more and more evident that the amount of time that staff are required to invest to complete annual health care

training requirements could almost add up to another full-time job. Organizations continue to evolve, technology continues to advance, and regulatory agencies continue to add requirements, and all of these things mean more hours allocated to staff training. To meet all of the necessary and growing demands, it is tempting to roll out violence prevention training purely to satisfy the regulatory requirements so staff can get back to doing their jobs. Although this approach may work for certain topics, this type of approach alone will never contribute to achieving a safe, violence-free workplace. Since WPV is such a complex issue, it requires a multifaceted approach to successfully mitigate it. WPVP training must be based on organizational statistics, trends, and needs, which likely requires it to be above and beyond just meeting the regulatory minimums. A fuller approach to violence prevention ensures a culture of safety, and not just one of "checking a box." In addition to reviewing stats, feedback from frontline staff often reveals patterns of concerns or pain points where they need support as well. Other issues surface that are not immediately obvious WPV issues, but definitely contribute to escalation when not addressed (i.e., visitor issues, patients recording staff with their phones, vaping in rooms, etc.). Updating policies/procedures to address these growing concerns not only gives staff guidance, but it allows them to feel empowered to tackle these issues. Keeping training relevant keeps interest and engagement high as well as creates a more robust program.

Solution: Center training around current data, trends, and deficiencies, as well as covering "requirements." Keep training relevant and up to date.

The factors below should be considered when deciding how to keep training relevant:

Training considerations:
- Conduct **rounding**/surveys and talk to staff to learn concerns, fears, and pain points.
- Review baseline data trends relative to location (hospital, ambulatory, department, etc.).

- Include training topics based on staff input and data trends, as well as topics that are regulatory requirements.
- Monitor data trends for improvements.
- Adapt policies/refresher training to address deficiencies or new concerns.

3. "More for Less" Approach

The expression, "You get what you pay for," is an accurate statement when it comes to investing in staff education. Of course, health care leaders want their staff to be safe; however, the large cost of training is often difficult to swallow. Building a comprehensive culture of violence awareness and prevention requires a financial investment, as well as a commitment to prioritize WPV initiatives. **Returns on investment (ROIs)** are not immediately obvious if the appropriate data is not being collected, crunched, and presented. Data shows that over time, the ROI in WPVP training outweighs the costs, proving that value is relative to spend. Adding up costs associated with staff morale, turnover, injuries, leave time, replacement costs, etc. due to a lack of violence prevention skill demonstrates the merit of investing in prevention instead. Although it is not always the easy thing to do, it is definitely the right thing to do for patients, visitors, providers, and employees. It benefits staff and patients alike, when staff become experts at recognizing escalating behaviors so they can communicate appropriately and build lasting rapport. It is also an opportunity for an organization to demonstrate their integrity, as it is also an investment in the overall patient experience.

Solution: Prioritize WPVP in the organization and develop a plan for funding training and initiatives.

The factors below should be considered when determining how to fund WPV training:

Training considerations:
- Make WPV a strategic initiative for the organization with tangible goals.
- Involve the Board of Directors/Board of Trustees to allocate funding annually.

- Build a budget/cost center specifically for WPV or add a line item in individual departmental budgets to cover costs.
- Get creative with funding. Work with the **Foundation** for the organization. Involve the community. Use a fundraising opportunity to support WPV needs and initiatives.
- Explore opportunities to apply for grants for safety research, quality, etc.
- Develop a multiyear plan to start small and add to the budget each year. (For more information on budgeting, refer to Chapter 5.)

4. "One and Done" Approach
There is a certain irony in wanting staff to have the very best skills and techniques available to be able to successfully manage upset individuals, all the while not wanting to allocate time for staff to be away from the "bedside" or from their daily tasks in order to develop those skills. It is critical for staff to be able to perform the job tasks that they were hired to do, so organizations need to afford them the opportunity to gain the skills needed, to be successful in their jobs. It is understood that staff's time is a precious commodity, especially when considering that training time is considered "nonproductive" time. But a true commitment to the organization's safety and well-being means allocating time toward continuous development and improvement. Competing priorities can often overshadow training as challenges emerge, but as staff's needs evolve, ongoing training is a must. There are a variety of approaches that can be implemented to better manage the work/training time balance, but it is essential that concepts are repeated, at least annually. Look for ways to incorporate informal, bite-sized trainings throughout the year to extend retention. Understanding where to taper training and how to tailor training will allow efficiencies to be built into the program so that more training exists in higher risk areas, as dictated by the needs within the organization. Staff training becomes useless if there is not a plan to sustain the philosophy and skills learned. Training is a process, not a one-time event.

Solution: Develop a sustainability plan for training. Incorporate several types of training to make training efficient and lasting.

The factors below should be considered when determining how to build sustainability into a WPV training program:

Training considerations:
- Assign responsibilities to a training coordinator.
- Consider purchasing a training program to meet needs.
- Consider training accessibility for all shifts/days of the week.
- Address the following factors in the education plan:
  - Varying class times for all shifts
  - Initial training plan versus continuing education/ refresher training plan
  - Formal training modalities versus informal training modalities
  - In-person options versus remote options
  - Full content for certification versus bite-size pieces for retention/reinforcement
  - Commercial program versus homegrown program
  - One-time topics versus ongoing topics (frequency of training)
  - Standardized consistent content versus custom/ refreshed content

5. "Not It" Approach
In order to meet expectations of governing agencies, it is natural to have a person assigned the responsibility to manage the WPVP program. But since a rich WPVP program requires the involvement of many different departments and job roles, no one singular person or department can "own" it. When responsibilities become stretched out over several areas, it is difficult to gain momentum, as each area has its own priorities. Furthermore, when a department needs to share the responsibility for WPV, but the WPV program "owner" has no authority over that department, the entire program can stall. It can be difficult to manage overall accountability for mitigating and eliminating violence when specific tasks become compartmentalized. This can be especially true when it comes to budgeting for WPV initiatives. What one department considers essential may not rank as high with the department that will need to budget for that task. This circumstance not only leaves the task incomplete but allows for

confusion about who is truly responsible for why the task remains unfinished. When there is a belief that "I'm not in charge of that" or "I can' do that right now," it can be detrimental to getting a program to take off. When so many people own a piece of the puzzle, there can be a mentality that "Preventing violence isn't my job. I only handle … (insert responsibility here)." The education and training staff may be "in charge of" the training program, but they are not responsible for unsuccessful de-escalation interventions. Compliance and safety staff are in charge of reducing numbers of violent injuries, yet they cannot affect any real change on the front lines as their scope of responsibility does not cover staff management. Risk Management staff are in charge of ensuring complete and clear data collection, but do not have the authority to ensure staff incident reporting is occurring after each incident. Facilities staff may feel they are not really responsible for violence prevention as they are only responsible for signage, lighting, door locks, etc. The question then asked is, "who is responsible for safety?" since no one feels it is them. When there is an assumption that managing violence is **Public Safety**'s job, staff never get the sense that they are all personally responsible. It is not just Public Safety's responsibility to keep people safe. It is everyone's responsibility. This belief demonstrates the critical need to have a highly engaged executive leader who will champion this cause and emphasize the importance of accountability across all departments. There must be a universal, basic understanding of personal accountability at the core of the organization, so that there will be a culture of personal responsibility in daily efforts (P.R.I.D.E.) (1). Otherwise, when determining who is responsible for violence and safety, there will be a resounding, "Not it."

Solution: Communicate the need for personal accountability at every level in order to create a culture of safety. Communication should be frequent and highly visible.

The following factors should be considered when determining how to instill accountability into a WPV training program:
- Assign respected authorities to this initiative.
- Have senior leaders round on units inquiring about safety.

- Prioritize incident reporting for staff with no repercussions.
- Address WPVP in management meetings.
- Create a campaign around violence reduction for staff.
- Offer staff resources for domestic violence, mental health support, de-escalation coaching, etc.
- Add goals/initiatives for WPV into performance reviews.
- Internally publish safety stories and celebrate successes of de-escalation.
- Empower staff to set limits and speak up.

Training is always a challenge, especially in health care, due to the high demands and extremely diverse locations and needs within the organization. Avoiding the five training program pitfalls listed earlier and working on the resolution strategies for each of these is a prescription for success when building or expanding a WPVP program. Being proactive by establishing a base plan that addresses engagement, executive financial support, staff needs, and training efficiencies will go a long way to ensuring an overall relevant and robust WPV program (Figure 6.1).

DO	DO NOT
✓ Create various training options	✗ "One Size Fits All" Approach
✓ Deliver training based on risk/need	✗ "Checking the Boxes" Approach
	✗ "More for Less" Approach
✓ Prioritize WPVP and construct a plan for budgeting	✗ "One and Done" Approach
	✗ "Not It" Approach
✓ Develop sustainability plan	
✓ Emphasize accountability	

Training Basics Do and Do Not

Figure 6.1: Training Basics—Do and Do Not

Determining Training Curriculum

Health care workers experience a wide range of WPV incidents of varying degrees, at a startling rate. Violence comes from patients, visitors, other health care workers, outsiders, and even leadership and peers. Violence prevention skills are essential but knowing what specific topics to train on can be challenging as WPV encompasses many variables. General staff awareness of the different types of WPV is the foundation of any program. Since violence can come from many different sources, start by identifying the potential ways staff can be exposed to violence. Gaining an understanding of the different types of violence will help shape the type of policies and training that will need to be developed. There are four types of WPV to consider.

Four Types of WPV (2)

> Type 1: Criminal Intent—Offender has no connection with the organization
>
> Type 2: Customer/Client—Offender is a patient, visitor, or customer of the organization
>
> Type 3: Worker-on-Worker—Offender is a current or former employee/affiliate of the organization
>
> Type 4: Personal Relationship—Offender has a relationship with an employee of the organization

These categories of WPV help outline training categories based on where potential violence comes from, and the level of risk that it creates.

WPV Type 1: Criminal Intent

Health care has been an increasing target for various types of violence. Since health care establishments are open to the public, often have large populations, and an open welcoming environment, it can be easy for criminals to exploit the opportunities these things present. Criminal activity can range from low, misdemeanor-type crimes, up to felonies and mass fatalities. Educating staff and providers on basic environmental awareness is helpful in creating a more secure and safe environment. Training on how to **"Harden the target"** can decrease crime and violence from offenders from outside of the organization. Training topics to mitigate Type 1 violence should include awareness about:

- Physical Security Awareness
- Theft Prevention (Prescription Pads, Meds, Staff Wallets/Purses, Food, etc.)
- Counterfeit Money

- Drug Activity
- Vehicle Theft (Theft from or Theft of Vehicles)
- Weapon Threats/Active Shooter

WPV Type 2 Customer/Client Violence

Various sources estimate that Type 2 violence accounts for over 90% of WPV in health care. Since this is so prevalent, the majority of training should focus on this level of violence. Verbal abuse, threats, and staff injuries from patients/visitors/families of patients may be a daily occurrence due to the high level of emotions and challenges in health care. Most WPV training programs utilize this component as the nucleus of their program, so a deeper look into the training for this level needs to occur. Building a robust training program around these concepts will prove to have the greatest impact in overall safety and culture in the organization. In addition to improving staff skills, other benefits include reduction in workplace injuries, higher morale, empowered staff, a cohesive team, and even improved patient experiences. Training topics to mitigate Type 2 violence should include:

- Awareness of internal WPV Policies and Programs
- Recognition of Escalating Behaviors
- Appropriate Responses for each Behavior Level
- Verbal Communication Techniques/De-escalation Training
- Physical Techniques (Disengagement, Escapes, Holds, etc.)
- Activation and Response to Emergency Codes
- Staff Empowerment to Speak Up
- Incident Reporting

These topics are the pedestals on which other initiatives and programs can be built. Not everyone in the organization needs to go through education for all of these topics though. Training should be based on role and location, as well as the type of work being conducted. Once risk of a particular area or role is determined, appropriate training can be assigned. A deeper look into the audience for each of these topics will be discussed in a later section.

Type 3: Worker-on-Worker Violence

Health care environments have diversified teams that need to work together. Although there are many benefits in having diverse teams, there can also be situations of harassment and bullying. "**Workplace bullying** is a persistent pattern of mistreatment from others in the workplace that causes either physical or emotional harm. It can include such tactics as verbal, nonverbal, psychological, and physical abuse, as well as humiliation" (2). In addition, bullying often includes misuse of power and authority. In a 2021 study by the Workplace Bullying Institute, it was determined that 73% of employees are aware of workplace bullying happening in their organization (3) (Figures 6.2 and 6.3).

Employed Americans: 39% suffer abusive conduct at work, another 22% witness it, 61% are affected by it, and 73% are aware that workplace bullying happens

Figure 6.2: Workplace Bullying Statistics (4)

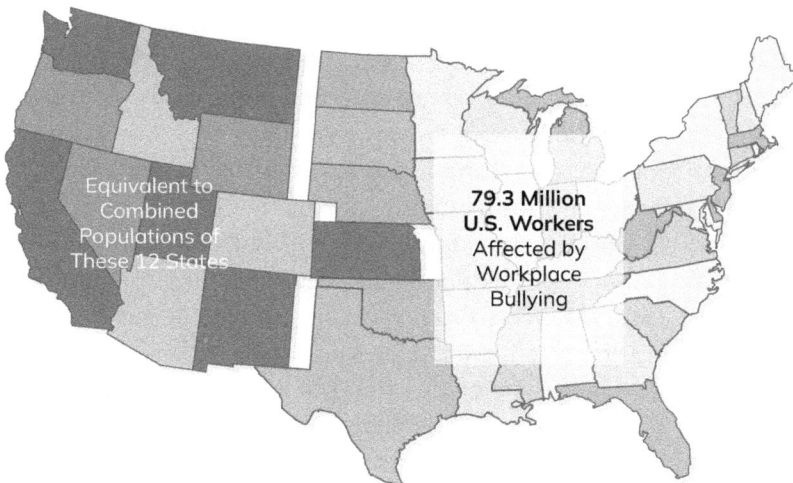

From the WBI 2021 U.S. Workplace Bullying Survey of Adult Americans

Equivalent to Combined Populations of These 12 States

79.3 Million U.S. Workers Affected by Workplace Bullying

Figure 6.3: U.S. Workplace Bullying Survey Results (5)

Health care teams are typically made up of several job types as well, with varying degrees of authority. Unfortunately, misuse of power can occur due to the natural hierarchy in the make-up of these teams. But bullying does not just occur by physicians, providers, or managers. Peer bullying is also prevalent. There are several professions that are notorious for "eating their young" when it comes to working with newer peers. This type of WPV tends to be the most invisible type of occurrence, and staff often suffer in silence. In order to combat this, staff need to be encouraged to accept individual differences. Training should be done to eliminate bias and honor cultural differences. Establishing inclusive workspaces creates high-performing teams. Training for Type 3 violence should include:

- Awareness of Policies Regarding Bullying/Harassment
- Education on Reporting without Repercussions
- Pathway for Communication about Abuse of Authority
- Unconscious Bias and Diversity Training
- Teamwork Training

Type 4: Personal Relationship Violence

Type 4 violence is based on domestic violence that spills over to the workplace. The offender is a spouse or partner of a staff member in the organization. So why is domestic violence an issue in the workplace? There are actually many reasons why this should be a concern. Recent statistics show that one in four women (25%) and one in nine men (11%) experience severe intimate partner physical violence, sexual violence, and/or partner stalking with injury (6). Health care is often a predominantly female population so almost 25% of staff could potentially be in harm's way. This type of violence does not stay contained at the home and can often result in harassing phone calls, unexpected visits to the workplace, as well as attempts to "create a scene" for the employee at work. Domestic violence is also a known cause for poor work performance, absenteeism, and increased health issues like depression, alcoholism, and other chronic medical conditions. Working to create a confidential and safe way for staff to get resources can be invaluable to the employee and to the organization. Training for Type 4 violence should include:

- Awareness of domestic violence policies and workplace support
- Resources for help/reporting
- Staff reminders about privacy—not giving out work schedules, phone numbers, etc.
- Proactive plan about when domestic violence is affecting the workplace
- Departmental training for partnership between Public Safety/Human Resources (active staff restraining orders, confidentiality, flexibility to protect and change predictable patterns)
  Additional concepts to consider for safety of the employee are:
  - Transfer to a different work location/department/role
  - Parking location and safety
  - Public Safety/team escorts for arrivals and departures from work
  - **Be on the Look Out (BOLO)** alerts for awareness in critical areas
  - Identifying worksite-specific actions that should be taken

Determining Risk Levels

Now that we have explored the various sources and types of violence, it is vital to determine which areas or which job roles should receive training, and what topics should be covered. Trying to determine which staff need WPV training can be quite complex. It is obvious that there can be a tenuous balance between the investment in training time and costs, and the benefit, value, and impact of the training. In addition, organizations must deliver training that meets the necessary regulatory requirements. There are many governmental or hospital accreditation agencies that must be taken into consideration when deciding specific training paths for staff. For example, in the United States, **The Joint Commission** specifies that annual WPVP training is required. The regulation is prescriptive in the training it requires and states that annual training must include verbal de-escalation, nonphysical intervention skills, physical intervention skills, and response to emergency codes for appropriate roles. The best way to determine how to assign education tracks to particular staff members is to assess the possible risk that they are exposed to based on their role and location/department. It is important to utilize existing organizational data to help determine which departments should be targeted. (For more information on data collection, refer to Chapter 4.) This data outlines which risk level (low, moderate, or high) should be assigned to each department, and then training can be tailored to the risk level.

Assigning training based on department risk level is an effective and appropriate approach. However, to maximize efficiency, further assessment can be done to break down training based on roles within each department. Not all staff have the same risk level within the same department. Crunching this data can be a daunting task when having to dial down to the individual job role, but it can be beneficial in reducing the training costs. One way to gain assistance with this task is to utilize an outside consultant. One such organization is the Crisis Prevention Institute (CPI). CPI offers a service in which they perform a free risk assessment for their clients using an algorithm to determine what type of training is needed based on the specific department, clientele, and job titles that exist in the organization. This evaluation can be useful to confirm internal estimations and could be a huge advantage in being able to take education tracks to the next level. Other considerations for determining risk could be if staff work alone, risk level of clientele/patients that they are treating, areas with verbal abuse via phone, etc.

How to Assign Risk

- Determine relevant criteria for baseline risk assessment (# of injuries, # of incidents, # of work days missed due to injuries, money spent on workplace compensation due to WPV injuries, etc.).
- Collect the data and organize it by department.
- Look for trends on which departments are at the top of each data set.
- Assign high-risk levels, moderate-risk levels, and low-risk levels based on the trends.
- Determine the education requirements and approach for each risk level.

- Continue to assess data regularly, and adjust training as needed, based on new data trends.

Examples of Low-Risk Departments:
- Business office staff
- Non-clinical areas (Marketing, Medical Records, etc.)
- Non-patient facing areas (Information Technology, Finance, etc.)

Examples of Moderate-Risk Departments:
- Ambulatory Site staff
- Clinical areas or patient facing areas (Phone Triage Nurses, Registrars, Clinical Nurses, Patient Care Technicians, etc.)
- Ancillary staff (Physical Rehab, Phlebotomy, Radiology, etc.)

Examples of High-Risk Departments:
- Emergency Department staff
- Critical Care staff
- Behavioral Health staff
- Public Safety staff

Required Training for Each Risk Level

Below are considerations for appropriate training topics based on risk levels (Figures 6.4 and 6.5).
Education for Staff in Low-Risk Areas should include:
- WPV Policies/Procedures
- How to Call for Help
- Emergency Code Response
- Incident Reporting
- Domestic Violence
- Staff Resources
- Active Weapon Threat

Education for Staff in Moderate-Risk Areas should include:
All of the previous topics in the low-risk category PLUS
- Recognition of Escalating Behaviors
- Stages of a Crisis

- Appropriate Approach for Each Behavior Level
- Possible Triggers
- Verbal Intervention Skills
- De-escalation Techniques

Education for Staff in High-Risk Areas should include:
All of the previous topics in the low-risk and moderate-risk categories PLUS

- Recognition of Escalating Behaviors
- Environmental Safety
- Physical Techniques (Disengagement, Escapes, Holds, etc.)
- Risks of Restraints
- Internal Response Teams
- Incident Follow-Up
- Consider Trauma-Informed Care

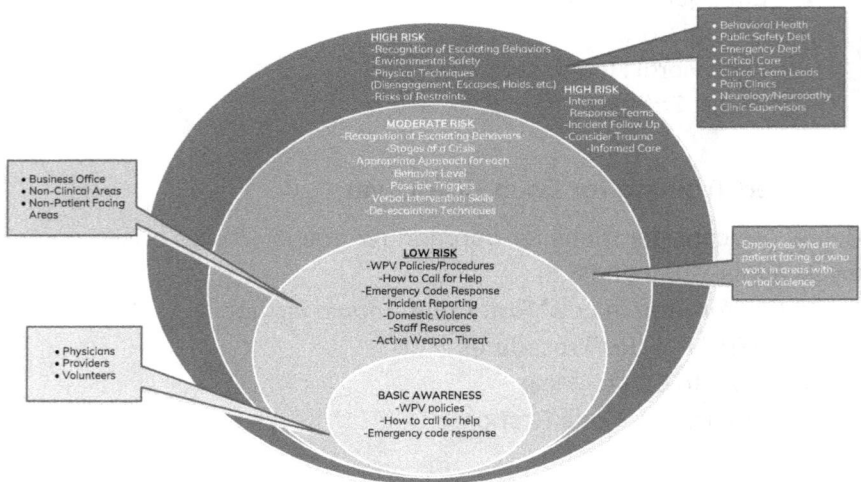

Figure 6.4: WPV Educational Topics Assigned by Risk Level and Job
*Note that each level of training needs to include the training topics for the levels below it as well.

Types of Training

Employing a wide variety of training modalities makes WPV education more efficient and effective. To reach multiple levels of staff, both clinical and non-clinical, the best practice is to utilize several different approaches in order to successfully implement a prevention program. There are two types of training platforms that can be utilized: Formal Training and Informal Training. Using a mix of training approaches will help keep training fresh while balancing the time commitment and content.

Formal Training consists of learning a specific, consistent curriculum that would result in a documented certification or completion. Formal training provides a structured approach and has specified objectives and goals. This type of learning program affords the opportunity for the instructors and facilitators to control the learning environment and experience. Each class offers every student the same content and works to obtain the same learning outcome. Formal training classes can be delivered by following an outline of a commercial program, or an internal, homegrown program.

Examples of formal training include:

- E-learning/Online Learning Modules
- Instructional Videos
- Workshops
- Webinars/Seminars
- Written Tests
- In-Person Classroom Style

Informal Training consists of learning that happens outside of a structured classroom environment, and although it can have intended objectives, it tends to have more unique learning outcomes for each student. Informal training can vary largely based on feedback and questions from attendees, as well as how they participate in the training. Informal training is often more flexible, ad hoc learning and can be just as valuable as formal training as it can assist with practical application and knowledge transfer to the real-world setting.

Examples of informal training include:

- Shift Huddles
- Self-Study
- Support Groups/Chat Groups
- In-services/Lunch and Learns
- Controlled Scenarios/Practical Application
- Live Action Drills

RISK LEVEL	Low Risk Areas (Hospital & Ambulatory)	Medium Risk Areas (Hospital & Ambulatory)	High Risk Areas (Hospital)	High Risk Areas (Ambulatory Sites)	Physicians/Providers
TARGET AUDIENCE	(All Employees) Employees in: Business Office Non-Clinical Areas Non-patient facing areas	Employees who are patient facing, or who work in areas with verbal violence	Employees in: • Behavioral Health • Public Safety Dept • Emergency Dept • Critical Care • Clinical Team Leads	Employees in: • Pain Clinics • Neurology/ Neuropathy • Clinic Supervisors • Behavioral Health	Non-employed Physicians and Providers (APNs, RN Practitioners, Physician Assistants, etc.)
TRAINING PROGRAM	Workplace Violence Awareness Online Learning (Homegrown)	CPI Online Module Prevention First or Verbal Intervention (Commercial Vendor)	CPI Not-Violent Crisis Intervention Certification May also consider Advanced Physical Techniques of Trauma Informed Care (Commercial Vendor) (CEUs granted)	CPI Non-Violent Crisis Intervention Certification (Commercial Vendor) (CEUs granted)	WPV Awareness for Providers Options to self-enroll in Prevention first (CEUs granted)
CONTENT INCLUDED:	-WPV Policies/ Procedures -How to Call for Help -Emergency Code Response -Incident Reporting -Domestic Violence -Staff Resources -Active Weapon Threat	Low Level Content PLUS -Recognition of Escalating Behaviors -Stages of a Crisis -Appropriate Approach for each Behavior Level -Possible Triggers -Verbal Intervention Skills -De-escalation Techniques	Low & Moderate Level Content PLUS -Environmental Safety -Physical Techniques (Disengagement, Escapes, Holds, etc.) -Risks of Restraints -Internal Response Teams -Incident Follow Up -Consider Trauma-Informed Care	Low & Moderate Level Content PLUS -Environmental Safety -Physical Techniques (Disengagement, Escapes, -Internal Response Teams -Incident Follow Up Consider Trauma-Informed Care	-WPV Policies/ Procedures -How to Call Help -Emergency Code Response -Incident Reporting -How to Support Staff

RISK LEVEL	Low Risk Areas (Hospital & Ambulatory)	Medium Risk Areas (Hospital & Ambulatory)	High Risk Areas (Hospital)	High Risk Areas (Ambulatory Sites)	Physicians/Providers
LENGTH OF TRAINING/ DELIVERY METHOD	10-15 Minutes Online	60 Minutes Online	8 Hours Classroom or Hybrid Version (4 Hours Online and 4 Hours Classroom)	8 Hours Classroom or Hybrid Version (4 Hours Online and 4 Hours Classroom)	60 Minutes Online
FREQUENCY OF TRAINING	Initially = <30 Days of Hire On-going = Annually	Initially = <30 Days of Hire On-going = Annually	Initially = 8 Hour Certification Annually = 4 Hour Refresher/Recert	Initially = 8 Hour Certification Annually = 4 Hour Refresher/Recert	Need it annually
REGULATORY REQUIREMENT	Mandatory Annually	Annual training is require based on job role	Annual training is required based on job role	Annual training is required based on job role	Annual training is required based on job role

Figure 6.5: Example of a WPV Education Plan (Utilizing the Crisis Prevention Institute programs)

Many opportunities exist for staff to hear the message about how to prevent WPV. Organizations should get creative with how and when they can educate their teams. Utilizing a variety of approaches prevents staff from getting bored and continues to keep topics fresh, while ensuring repeated exposure to the content. This is the best way for staff to remember what they were taught and find ways to incorporate it into their daily practice.

Working to outline the type of WPV training needed and the specifics about who should receive it will be the foundation of a WPV training program. Then, by tailoring the topics and utilizing a variety of training modalities, organization will be able to provide efficient and cost-effective training options. These strategies can start small and can occur in steps, working toward a larger, overall education plan for the organization. Once an organization commits to following these steps, they will be able to build a robust and successful WPVP training program.

References

1. Bimm, Greg. 1987. *Personal Responsibility in Daily Efforts (P.R.I.D.E.).* Personal.
2. Centers for Disease Control and Prevention. 2020. "Workplace Violence Prevention for Nurses." *Centers for Disease Control and Prevention,* February 7, 2020. https://wwwn.cdc.gov/WPVHC/Nurses/Course/.
3. Namie, Gary. 2022. "2021 WBI U.S. Workplace Bullying Survey." *Workplacebullying.org.* Accessed February 28, 2022. https://workplacebullying.org/2021-wbi-survey/.
4. Namie, Gary. 2022. "Workplace Bullying Institute—All Things Workplace Bullying." Accessed March 5, 2022. https://workplacebullying.org/wp-content/uploads/2021/04/2021-Full-Report.pdf.
5. Namie, Ruth, and Gary Namie. 2022. "Workplace Bullying Institute Study 2021." *Workplacebullying.org.* Accessed March 7, 2022. https://workplacebullying.org/2021-wbi-survey/.
6. National Coalition Against Domestic Violence (NCADV). 2022. "The Nation's Leading Grassroots Voice on Domestic Violence." Accessed March 14, 2022. https://ncadv.org/.

Glossary of Terms

Be on the Look Out (BOLO) An alert or broadcast, often issued by Public Safety, to alert others about a suspicious or wanted person or vehicle. A BOLO typically contains descriptive, identifying information and a phone number to call if the person or vehicle is observed.

Formal Training A learning session that has specific, consistent curriculum that would result in a documented certification or completion. Formal training provides a structured approach and has the same specified objectives and goals for each student.

Foundation A nonprofit organization that supports the programs and services of a local hospital. They operate independently from the hospital and have their own focus and goals, with the primary goal of raising money for its affiliate hospital(s) and to increase community awareness.

Harden the Target A term meaning to strengthen the security of a building or area in order to increase protection and remove or reduce opportunities of crime and violence. Examples of target hardening techniques can include physical modifications, such as secure locks and motion lights, as well as procedural elements like visitor screenings and general access control.

Informal Training A learning session that happens outside of a structured classroom environment, and although it can have intended objectives, it tends to have more unique learning outcomes for each student.

Public Safety A department in a health care system that has a broad span of responsibilities, some of which include managing safety and security incidents, responding to emergency incidents, de-escalating verbal and physical disturbances, assisting with keeping patients safe, handling credentialing and identification of staff, and managing parking responsibilities. Sometimes referred to as the "Security" or "Protection" Department.

Returns on Investment (ROI) A performance measure used to evaluate the efficiency or profitability of a program. ROI measures the program value or benefits, relative to the investment costs.

Rounding Walking through workplace departments to regularly check in with employees (similar to medical staff making patient rounds). It can be used to assess morale, demonstrate engagement, confirm compliance, etc.

The Joint Commission The oldest and largest U.S. standards-setting and accrediting body in health care; an independent, not-for-profit organization in the United States that administers voluntary accreditation programs for hospitals and other health care organizations. A majority of U.S. state governments recognize The Joint Commission accreditation as a condition of licensure in order to receive governmental insurance reimbursements. The Joint Commission drives quality improvement and patient safety in health care through accreditation, certification, regulatory standards, and measurement and performance improvement areas. Previously called Joint Commission on Accreditation of Health care Organizations (JCAHO), The Joint Commission accredits approximately 88% of U.S. hospitals (4477 hospitals) and 22,000 total U.S. health care organizations and programs.

Workplace Bullying A persistent pattern of mistreatment from others in the workplace that causes either physical or emotional harm. It can include such tactics as verbal, nonverbal, psychological, and physical abuse, as well as humiliation.

Workplace Violence (WPV) Any act or threat of physical violence, harassment, intimidation, or other threatening disruptive behavior that occurs at the work site.

Workplace Violence Prevention (WPVP) A system of attitudes, strategies, practices, initiatives, and behaviors that work to stop and prevent any acts of threat, harassment, intimidation, or disruptive behavior from occurring at a place of employment.

CHAPTER 7

Building a Culture of Violence Prevention

Kimberly A. Urbanek

CPI

Objectives

After reading this chapter, one should be able to:

- Understand how to build sustainability with a culture of violence prevention
- Identify and mitigate barriers to sustainability
- Know how to use change management to advance workplace violence prevention
- Understand how to implement changes that stay

The ultimate sign of successful implementation of a program occurs when classroom strategies and boardroom concepts are practiced and applied in real-world situations daily, and are producing desired, positive outcomes. Sustainability of a **workplace violence prevention (WPVP)** program is essential to affect any real change. Even after developing policies, meeting regulatory standards, engaging leadership, establishing training programs, capturing statistics, and creating committees, violence prevention **culture** does not just automatically surface. A true culture of violence prevention cannot be created by just following the above steps. It must become part of an organization's culture to have a lasting impact.

Sustaining a WPV Program by Building the Culture

Culture is defined as a set of shared attitudes, values, goals, and practices that characterize an institution or organization. Simply put, the culture of the organization is reflected in the behaviors of the team and the way that things are done. But changing a culture is difficult at its best and seemingly impossible at its worst. Cultural values are buried deep within the organization and are driven by the individuals who work there. Staff tend to hold tightly to their way of doing things, so how can an organization make a sustainable WPVP program and truly make it last? There are several steps that can be taken to move your WPVP program to the next level, so that safety and prevention are not just initiatives but are woven into the fabric of the organization.

The culture of an organization can be compared to an iceberg (Figure 7.1). About 90% of an iceberg sits below the water and is unseen. In order to visibly change staff behaviors and norms, leaders need to discover and manage the values, attitudes, and assumptions that are built over time, which are often not outwardly visible upon first look.

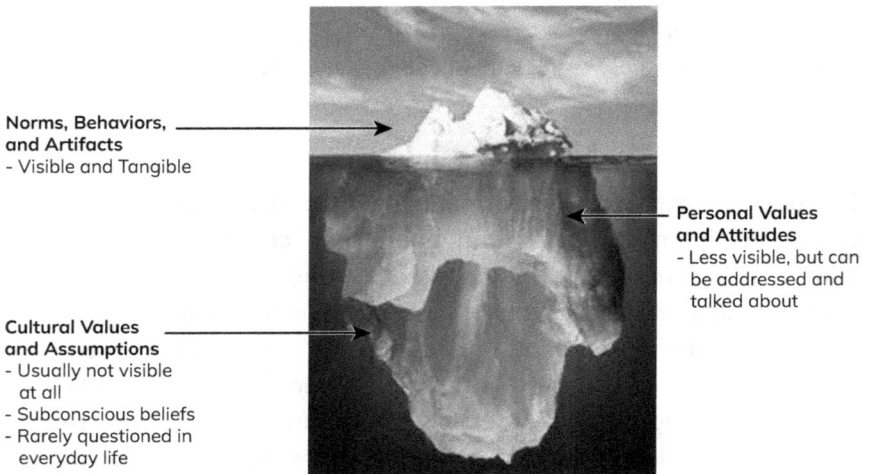

Norms, Behaviors, and Artifacts
- Visible and Tangible

Personal Values and Attitudes
- Less visible, but can be addressed and talked about

Cultural Values and Assumptions
- Usually not visible at all
- Subconscious beliefs
- Rarely questioned in everyday life

Figure 7.1: The Culture Iceberg (1). Photo by: Ralph A. Clevenger

Barriers to Sustainability

First, recognize that at the core, making an impact with your WPVP program is about **change management**. Since emotion, aggression, and violence are so historically imbedded in health care experiences, it is important to understand that this implementation must not be the next superficial, "flavor of the month" type of initiative or project. This is a culture change. Previously held beliefs will need to be challenged and amended. One such area is around beliefs about reporting **workplace violence (WPV)** incidents. Studies show that there are multiple barriers to staff reporting that need to be addressed to understand the obstacles to implementing this culture change. Below are some of the ingrained beliefs that may halt the drive to improve WPV.

Underlying Beliefs Affecting Reporting/Prohibiting Culture Change (2):

- Incidents are underreported by staff/do not know what to report
- No formal reporting mechanism or no clear reporting policy
- Inconsistencies in violence definitions
- Staff feeling that violence is "just part of the job"
- Staff perception that they will not be supported (Focus on "Customer is always right")
- Staff feeling that nothing will be done/lack of action; no follow-up from reporting
- Staff tend to report incidents based on severity or if there was an injury
- Staff choose not to report based on the patient's clinical condition (if there is a perception that the violence was unintentional or if the patient did not "know better")
- Staff think someone else probably reported it
- Reporting is complicated or time consuming

It is obvious how some of the above-stated beliefs are contradictory to new prevention ideas that an organization wants staff to adopt. By understanding "why" staff aren't reporting, underlying beliefs will surface and can be addressed directly. It is imperative to learn the current culture first to better learn what direction it needs to be steered.

Change Management

Next, organizations need to follow a plan for change management to adjust the culture. This is essential for sustainability. Change management is the practice and process of supporting people through change, with the goal of ensuring that the change is successful in the long term. Change management helps people to change their behaviors, attitudes, and/or work processes to achieve a desired business objective or outcome (3). It should be noted that change management is quite different from project management. WPVP cannot be a "project." A project has a completion date, whereas a WPVP will never be "finished." A project requires a person, or group of people to complete certain tasks by a specific deadline, while being on time and on budget. Change management actually focuses on helping employees manage the disruption they experience during the change, while working to remove obstacles and add improvements to sustain the change (3). There are many techniques and strategies that an organization can choose from to assist them in implementing this change. These methods vary and may have as few as three steps or as many as ten steps to follow, but there are a lot of common components between them. Below are some essential pieces to consider when working to successfully alter the culture of an organization:

- Leadership—Consists of engaging leadership and necessary decision makers (creating policies, standards, strategies, goals, etc.)
- Communication—Consists of multiple, repeat layers of communication to inform staff and other stakeholders about plans and expectations; focus on positivity and need
- Engagement—Consists of connecting to purpose and value of program; collecting feedback and listening to concerns; engaging early adopters and uniting others to the common goal; building relationships
- Planning and Design—Consists of analysis of current workflow and evaluation of how to integrate new initiatives; identify barriers and work out logistics to implementation
- Training—Consists of guiding and educating staff and role-specific rollout and ongoing, follow-up training; ensure training shows up in daily practices
- Review—Consists of evaluating program success, measuring performance, tracking progress, and reviewing and monitoring participation and feedback

Whatever change management tool is used to prepare the organization and staff for this plan of action, it is important to remember that not everyone will respond the same way. There will need to be consideration for the different members of the organization. For example, the communication and information that will go out to staff will need to have a different look when targeting providers and physicians. Tailoring the change information to the specific audience allows organizations to gain buy-in and hear concerns early. Feedback, both positive and negative, will allow organizations to plan solutions and pull in others to help champion the program rollout. For the program to flourish, each individual is going to need to recognize their part of the responsibility to move the initiative forward. Individual accountability is essential to incorporating violence prevention into the culture of an organization and a lack of accountability damages the team. "Accountability in the workplace means that all employees are responsible for their actions, behaviors, performance and decisions. It's also linked to an increase in commitment to work and employee morale, which leads to higher performance. It's recognizing that other team members and general company performance depend on the results of your work. When employees are held accountable, they take responsibility for results and don't assume it's someone else's job" (4).

Leadership

The right leaders need to be involved in the development of a WPVP culture. This leadership group must be multidisciplinary and interdepartmental. There needs to be consideration about which leader is best to engage physicians and providers as well, as they must be part of the solution. Physicians/providers may present unique challenges but there must be a plan to bring them along. Occasionally, organizations will find that some of the doctors have a history of bullying or degrading staff. Leadership must double down on demonstrating to staff that they should not tolerate these poor behaviors and show they are addressing all forms of WPV. Some physicians may simply not have access to WPVP training or may not be required to take training as part of their contract. These issues must be remediated so they do not erode the foundation of violence prevention that an organization is creating.

One mistake that an organization can make is trying to make a cultural transformation into a marketing project where there is a lot of initial attention and focus, but then the interest dies down. The WPVP program needs to continue to be a strategic goal, even in the face of other competing priorities. It is easy to live by values when situations are ideal. However, it is during challenging times that values get pushed aside for other priorities. In health care there are real issues that easily distract from focus on the WPV program. A staffing crisis, a merger, financial challenges, a pandemic, leadership changes, or other regulatory demands may attempt to edge out the importance of WPVP. It is during these unprecedented times that leadership must continue the work to not abandon their efforts to move the WPV program forward.

Communication

As mentioned, communication is the cornerstone to expanding and improving the WPVP program. There are many creative and practical ways to inform and motivate staff around this topic. Communication must be frequent and consistent. Vary the format to keep information fresh for staff and to reach the highest number of staff. Start with opportunities that are already in place such as e-mail, newsletters, organizational web pages, department meetings, and shift change huddles. Continue to add to these methods. Institute leadership rounding. Host a Townhall meeting for staff. Hold a lunch and earn session for staff to attend during their breaks. Perform a staff survey about WPV. All of these are ways to reiterate the need for a culture of violence prevention and staff accountability. Below are additional ways to continue to keep WPVP culture highly visible.

- Identify a department to pilot new initiatives. Get their feedback and review the outcomes. Share their successes and lessons learned with other departments and expand the initiatives to full implementation. This gives staff a sense of ownership since the project they were a part of is now part of the entire organization.
- Develop a Safety Champion program. Select individuals from every area to represent the frontline staff and to be the department "experts" on all things WPV.

- Find ways to incorporate staff feedback and publicly address staff concerns.
- Hang a Safety Tracking board in high-risk departments as a daily, visible reminder of the goal of safety for every employee. Keep track of how many safe days have accrued without an injury due to violence.
- Hold a community awareness event or fundraiser. Communities often look for ways to help local clinicians. Proceeds can go toward training budget or physical security needs to make staff safer while at work.
- Hold a panel interview with Public Safety, Risk Management, Legal, and Occupational Safety. Allow staff to ask questions that they have had no other venue to ask.
- Partner with local law enforcement for training drills, collaboration, and validation for WPV policies.

Staff Engagement

Staff engagement is critical to success. Staff must continually be reminded of initiatives in order to get them to believe in the goal. One approach to enhance staff engagement is to use the Diffusion of Innovation (DOI) Behavioral Change Model developed by Everette M. Rogers (Figure 7.2) (5). In this model, Rogers outlines five categories of adopters. The categories of adopters are: innovators, early adopters, early majority, late majority, and laggards. Using this model has proven to be successful at getting the majority of staff to engage and buy-in by focusing on the innovators and early adopters first, with the goal of attracting the early majority. The early adopters are the people who are willing and excited to participate in innovation. The early majority are more likely to adopt new processes after they see and hear others have already done it. Since early adopters are opinion leaders, their support will influence the early majority to come aboard, which gives the tipping point of over 50% of staff engaged (6).

Planning and Design

Allowing staff to be part of the planning process is a great way to identify potential risks and consequences of new initiatives, while providing staff a sense of control over their personal safety at work. Develop

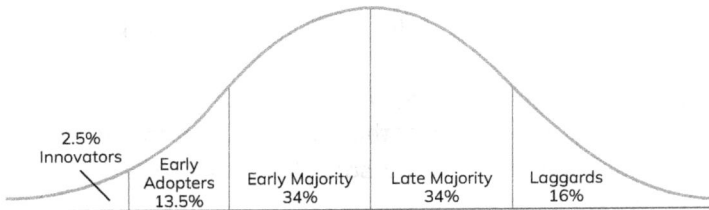

There are five established adopter categories:

1. Innovators – (2.5%) These are people who want to be the first to try the innovation. They are venturesome and interested in new ideas. These people are very willing to take risks and are often the first to develop new ideas. Very little, if anything, needs to be done to appeal to this population.

2. Early Adopters – (13.5%) These are people who represent opinion leaders. They enjoy leadership roles and embrace change opportunities. They are already aware of the need to change and so are very comfortable adopting new ideas. Strategies to appeal to this poopulation include how-to manuals and information sheets on implementation. They do not need information to convince them to change.

3. Early Majority – (34%) These are people are rarely leaders, but they do adopt new ideas before the average person. That said, they typically need to see evidence that the innovation works before they are willing to adopt it. Strategies to appeal to this population include success stories and evidence of the innovation's effectiveness

4. Late Majority – (34%) These people are skeptical of change and will only adopt an innovation after it has been tried by the majority. Strategies to appeal to this population include information on how many other people have tried the innovation and have adopted it successfully.

5. Laggards – (16%) These people are bound by tradition and very conservative. They are very skeptical of change and are the hardest group to bring on board. Strategies to appeal to this population include statistics, fear appeals, and pressure from people in the other adopter groups.

Figure 7.2: DOI Behavioral Change Model Developed by Everette M. Rogers (5)

initiatives that address real and relevant issues on a unit. Solutions to these problems are mutually beneficial and quickly connect staff to the purpose. Since patient violence (Type 2 violence) is the greatest risk, conduct department-level focus groups to determine the most common causes. These focus groups often uncover more questions initially but result in great wins. Process failures and procedural shortcomings are revealed, shining a light on issues that may be causing unnecessary escalation.

Consider This Scenario

Focus group conducted with Labor and Delivery staff
Leadership from the Department of Labor and Delivery did not know if WPVP training was necessary for their team. Often, the birth of a baby is a happy and joyous occasion, and the department has a low rate of injury due to violence. However,

during focus group meetings, when asking about the most common situations that cause upset in their unit, there was a clear answer among all clinical team members regarding a necessary procedure after birth. After an infant is born, they need to receive a critical **Vitamin K** injection to prevent excessive bleeding in the infant. The family has the option to refuse the injection, which many families initially opt for. However, if a family refuses the injection, law requires that Infant Protection Services be immediately notified as the injection is deemed so critical to life and safety that this refusal is seen as neglect. Of course, immediately upon learning that they will be reported for neglect of their baby, families escalate from confusion, to yelling, swearing, and screaming. This scenario should not be unfolding on the day of the infant's birth but should be embedded into the pre-birthing process. It should be discussed at every physician appointment, along with appropriate options, and should not be left as a surprise message for nurses to deliver. This upset is a perfect example of a process failure that creates a pain point that can be eliminated, to make staff safer in their workplace.

Training

As staff begin to embrace and absorb the WPVP philosophy, it will be necessary to provide tools and tips for staff to put the prevention techniques into their everyday practice. This is called **training transfer** and is above and beyond other training modules. WPV awareness is not enough. Staff need to be skilled in de-escalation and service recovery. However, as important as de-escalation is, it is still a reactive measure. Ultimately, staff should be proactive in identifying possible upset early and preventing escalation from even occurring. Building common language throughout the organization and providing usable strategies and techniques will empower staff to grow and manage situations with expertise. (Refer to Chapter 10 for ideas on training transfer.)

In addition to honing their interventions, staff also need to reflect on their own personal triggers and where they may fall short in maintaining their composure. Although staff cannot control the behaviors of other people, they can control how they respond to those behaviors. When staff have repeat exposure to violence, they can become desensitized and develop compassion fatigue. This stress may result in them being reactionary and unintentionally argumentative with patients. Staff need to learn their own limits and not respond to provocations. Developing resourcefulness and resilience in staff ensures that they can maintain professionalism. Staff need to be supported in recognizing when they need to step away momentarily to regain their own self-control. Staff develop a strong sense of personal ownership over their safety when they learn ways to manage escalation while still feeling in control of their own behaviors and reactions. (Refer to Chapter 10 for ideas on identifying personal triggers.)

Review

Organizations need to conduct ongoing reviews of their WPV program. Continuous evaluation will allow organizations to analyze changes in statistics, identify if programs are yielding desired outcomes, and elicit staff feedback about any obstacles or unintended consequences. It will be important to adjust or change initiatives to better align with the organizational goals as more is learned. Organizations should also examine the benefits gained through these improvements versus the cost of implementation. Reevaluating the culture and how it impacts staff will provide insight into the success of the program. Organizations should see reductions in injuries, negative psychological impact, turnover, cost of lost time, and compassion fatigue. Organizations should find value in and celebrate investments in staff debriefings, positive reinforcement of successful interventions, and solutions that are developed to troubleshoot barriers. All of these positive findings will continue to strengthen the idea that WPVP needs to continue to be a strategic priority. Through regular assessments, organizations can continue to improve and grow their WPV program and prevent recurring incidents.

Once WPVP is woven into the daily efforts of an organization, a culture of prevention will be prevalent and will sustain the growth of the WPV program. Connecting appropriate leadership with engaged staff creates the foundation of the program. Initiatives can continue to advance as staff start implementing prevention strategies as part of their routine interactions. A proactive approach to WPV becomes the culture of the organization and serves as the best prevention method to mitigate violence and keep staff, patients, and families as safe as possible.

References

1. Ilaydacemoglu. 2016. "Cultural Iceberg." Organizational Culture Blog. Graduate Students and Faculty of UAlbany's Department of Communication, December 15, 2016. https://orgcultureblog.wordpress.com/2016/12/15/cultural-iceberg/.
2. Blando, James, Marilyn Ridenour, Daniel Hartley, and Carri Casteel. 2015, January. "Barriers to Effective Implementation of Programs for the Prevention of Workplace Violence in Hospitals." *Online Journal of Issues in Nursing* 20 (1): 5. U.S. National Library of Medicine. https://www.ncbi.nlm.nih.gov/pmc/articles/PMC4719768/.
3. Pan American Health Organization, and World Health Organization. 2019. "Change Management in Public Health." Understanding Change Management in Public Health – Version 1.0. United States Agency for International Development (USAID), the Government of Canada and the Spanish Agency for International Development Cooperation (AECID), Department of Evidence and Intelligence for Action in Health, August 2019. https://www3.paho.org/ish/images/toolkit/IS4H-KCCM-EN.pdf.
4. Amin, Hiba. 2022. "How to Make Accountability a Core Part of Your Workplace Culture." *Hypercontext*, February 2, 2022. https://hypercontext.com/blog/management-skills/create-culture-accountability-workplace.
5. Rogers, Everette M. 2019. "Diffusion of Innovation Theory." *Behavioral Change Models*, September 9, 2019. https://sphweb.bumc.bu.edu/otlt/mph-modules/sb/behavioralchangetheories/behavioralchangetheories4.html.
6. Sinek, Simon. 2010. "How to Make a Cultural Transformation | Simon Sinek." *YouTube*, January 10, 2020. https://www.youtube.com/watch?v=N9d0NqSztWA.

Glossary of Terms

Change management The practice and process of supporting and helping people change their behaviors, attitudes, and/or work processes to achieve a desired business objective or outcome, with the goal of ensuring that it is successful long term.

Culture A set of shared attitudes, values, goals, and practices that characterize an institution or organization.

Training Transfer Applying knowledge and skills acquired during training to a targeted job or role; practical application of gained knowledge to real-life work scenarios

Vitamin K An essential vitamin needed by the human body that plays a key role in helping blood blot to prevent excessive bleeding.

Workplace Violence (WPV) Any act or threat of physical violence, harassment, intimidation, or other threatening disruptive behavior that occurs at the work site.

Workplace Violence Prevention (WPVP) A system of attitudes, strategies, practices, initiatives, and behaviors that work to stop and prevent any acts of threat, harassment, intimidation, or disruptive behavior from occurring at a place of employment.

CHAPTER 8

The Balancing Act between Patient Advocacy and Staff Support

Lindsey Harrington

Objectives

After reading this chapter you should be able to:

- Identify ways to communicate a workplace violence prevention culture to staff
- Understand how to build a collaborative relationship between staff and customers
- Know how to empower staff and allow exceptions without undermining them
- Identify ways that leaders can support staff and restore a sense of safety after a workplace violence incident
- Understand the need to provide emotional support to staff following workplace violence

It used to be uncommon to hear about situations of violence in schools and workplaces, but unfortunately, the number of reports of aggression and outright violence in the places we work has been dramatically increasing. This has led to organizations wondering how to create a culture of safety in their workplaces to keep both their customers and staff safe. Creating a culture of safety for your organization requires a mutual commitment to staff and customers to have a healthy nonviolent relationship. When thinking about **workplace violence** (WPV) it could be easy to lose sight of the importance of patient experience. This would be a huge mistake. When organizations focus on enhancing the patient experience, the likelihood of patients becoming agitated or disgruntled is reduced, in turn reducing the chances of WPV. This chapter serves as a resource for how to find balance between expectations for good customer service while supporting your employees to create a healthy and safe work environment.

Creating and Communicating a Culture of Safety

Creating a culture of safety involves communicating to both the customers and staff working for the organization that any forms of aggression or violence are unacceptable and will be treated with the seriousness they demand. The expectation for the environment and behavior of those in the space to engage in nonviolent, cooperative behavior is often presented through a variety of communication mediums including but not limited to signage, formal policies and procedures, and the response from representatives of the organization when differences arise.

Signage

One of the most obvious ways to communicate your organization's stance on violence in the workplace is through signage declaring your commitment to a safe, nonviolent environment. Similar to the way that the pictures chosen to be hung in a waiting room or the graphics on an organization's website set the tone for what to expect, signs communicate the organization's stance on safety in the workplace and set expectations for both customers and staff (Figure 8.1). Having signs in highly visible places demonstrates that safety is a top priority for the organization. When identifying locations for signage, consider points of access, visibility, and where violence is most likely to occur. Most organizations utilize their reception area or waiting room to display culture of safety signs as this is the first point of contact with customers. Waiting rooms offer the opportunity for a captive audience to read material as a commitment to their safety and a forewarning that aggressive behavior will not be tolerated. **Culture of safety signage** is especially important in areas where wait times may be long or hard to anticipate (e.g., emergency rooms, doctor's offices, service centers) as this can result in impatient customers and increased chances of aggression. When situations begin to escalate, it is helpful to staff to be able to point to signs as a gentle reminder that violence is unacceptable in this environment. The language selected for culture of safety signage should also be gentle, positive, and respectful. It is also advised to focus language on behavior that is expected rather than a negative tone in detailing unacceptable behaviors.

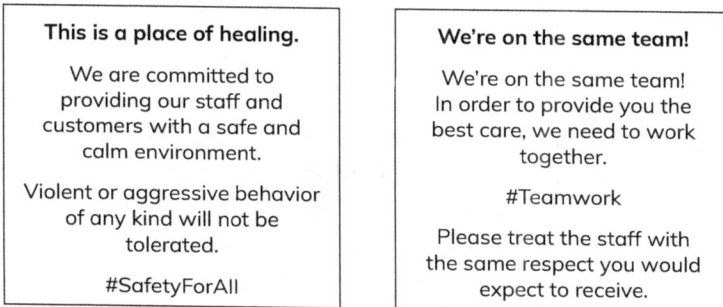

This is a place of healing. We are committed to providing our staff and customers with a safe and calm environment. Violent or aggressive behavior of any kind will not be tolerated. #SafetyForAll	**We're on the same team!** We're on the same team! In order to provide you the best care, we need to work together. #Teamwork Please treat the staff with the same respect you would expect to receive.

Figure 8.1: Examples of Culture of Safety Signage

Formal Policies and Procedures

In addition to signage, the paperwork and policies of an organization convey information about their culture of safety. Organizations that require their clients to complete paperwork or sign consent upon admission should incorporate into their admission packet information about the organization's safety policies and expectations. This helps to set expectations around appropriate communication and behavior as groundwork for the relationship between the customer and the organization. Having policies in place and going over these policies at the onset of treatment/service allows staff to set clear expectations up front and forewarn of consequences if violence is encountered. Formal policies should outline what constitutes WPV (e.g., verbal aggression, threats, intimidating behavior, physical violence, sexual comments, destruction of property, etc.) as well as possible repercussions for such behaviors (e.g., cancellation of appointment, termination of services, **behavioral contracts**/agreements). Policies allow for organizations to have clear ramifications for inappropriate behavior in the workplace and decrease the likelihood of subjective, and potentially discriminatory, applications of consequences.

Clear Communication

Most policy conflicts between customers and staff come from a break-down in communication. Therefore, one of the simplest ways to prevent conflict between staff trying to adhere to policies and customer's dis-agreement is to make sure that policies and procedures are clear from the start. Making sure that both customers and staff are accurately informed of the current policies helps everyone be on the same page and tends to dissolve a fair portion of potential conflict. This can be particularly difficult if policies change frequently (e.g., visitation rules/guidelines during COVID-19 pandemic). When policies are updated or changed, it is critical that staff and customers are informed as soon as possible to reduce the chances of confusion and agitation. In situations where there is a disagreement, the first step is to identify the break-down in communication and to clarify the standing policy. Once the current practice is identified, gentle explanation of the policy/procedure should be shared and explained to the customer. It is not helpful to say who was "right," as this continues to put the customer and staff member on opposing sides, perpetuating conflict. Instead, simply state the policy as it currently exists and offer an opportunity for further clarifying questions. It can be helpful to provide the policy in writing, as well as verbally inform the customer. Additionally, it is important to acknowledge that getting misinformation can be frustrating. Validat-ing this experience can go a long way in repairing any disruption in the relationship, between the customer and the organization. Anytime a difference in opinions occur, it is important to engage in clarifying conversations with **soft language**, to reduce chances of violence and aggression (Figure 8.2).

Scenario: Customer believes that the visiting hours are from 12 pm to 5 pm. The staff member believes the hours are from 12 pm to 4 pm and asks the customer to leave because it is past visitation. Customer becomes upset and refuses to leave. Staff confirms that the hours are from 12 pm to 4 pm, per the current visitor guidelines.

Staff response: *"I'm sorry for the confusion. Here is the flyer with the current visitor guidelines that was just updated on Monday. It states that the visiting hours are from 12 pm to 4 pm today. I'm sure this must be frustrating as you thought you would have more time with your loved one. You can take this flyer with you to have the visiting schedule as reference for your next visit."*

Figure 8.2: Example of Clear Communication and Use of Soft Language

Soft Language

We are social creatures and more suggestible to the behavior of others than one might realize. Consider this: Have you ever heard that yawns are "contagious"? From a biological perspective, there is truth to this. Yawns occur not only because we are tired but also when our brains are not getting enough oxygen. A yawn is essentially a deep breath that allows the brain to get more oxygen quickly. When we see someone else yawn, it triggers a subconscious survival response for us to also yawn, because if the yawner in the same room as us is not getting enough oxygen, we instinctively worry we might need more oxygen too. So, we yawn. This is an example of humans subconsciously **mirroring** others' behaviors. Another way we mirror others' behavior is by matching their volume and tone of voice. If someone is angry and yelling at you, there is an instinctual pull to match the emotion of the aggressor. Their voice goes up in volume, and we want to raise our voices to match. They speak faster, you speak faster. The problem with mirroring in aggressive situations is that it results in increased verbal aggression and increases the risk of violence. Therapists have figured out how to use subconscious mirroring in reverse, to de-escalate high-emotion situations. Instead of mirroring an angry client, therapists do the opposite—they lower the volume of their voice and slow down their rate of speech. This helps to de-escalate the agitated individual, as they are also pulled to match the behavior of the calm therapist. By consciously controlling the volume, tone, and rate of speech, therapists can subconsciously influence de-escalation.

Communicating the importance of soft language to staff is a useful tool in de-escalating aggression in the workplace. When talking with someone who is upset, it is important to be mindful of the volume, tone, rate, and choice of words, to create a safe, calm environment. For most people, word choice tends to be the only focus when communicating during difficult situations, but this is a mistake as content is actually the smallest part of the message getting communicated. According to Albert Mehrabin's 7-38-55 Rule of Personal Communication (1), only 7% of the message that an individual receives is determined by the actual words that are communicated. This means that 93% of the message being conveyed is expressed through **paraverbal** (tone, pitch, volume, and rate) and **nonverbal communication** (body language, personal space, and physical environment). Therefore, while it is still important to carefully consider the words we choose when communicating to someone who is upset, even more critical is the way the message is delivered. Best practice for situations of WPV recommends using soft and compassionate language.

Soft language includes using a gentle tone of voice that is understanding, compassionate, and supportive. It can be helpful to think about how you would communicate respectfully and kindly to a loved one (e.g., your grandmother, small child). Volume should be set slightly lower than normal speaking volume. When we lower our volume, it encourages the other person to focus in when listening to hear your message. It is also more difficult to continue yelling when the other person is not engaging, because the quiet voice does not match or return the energy. Rate (or speed) of speech should be slightly slower than a normal pace. (NOTE OF CAUTION: Be careful not to speak too slowly though as this can be perceived as being condescending.) When emotions are high, it becomes more difficult for the emotional individual to process information quickly. Communicating at a slower rate makes it easier for the emotional person to process the information and decreases the likelihood of missing important parts of the content being conveyed.

Building Collaborative Relationships

One way to prevent conflict between staff and customers is to focus on aligning common goals and mutual expectations. Aggression and escalation of violence often occur because there is a misconception that only one side can "win" the disagreement. When one side wins, and the other loses, the organization loses. This mentality of needing to be right is a problem that must be corrected, as it is a common, and often avoidable source of WPV. Since organizations exist to serve customers, and customers need organizations for services, there is a need to coexist. It is important in situations of disagreement, to look for opportunities to be on the same side, so that both parties "win."

Cooperation and Collaboration

One way that organizations get caught up in being "right" is when staff seek compliance rather than cooperation. Compliance implies "you do what I say, no questions asked," which automatically establishes a power imbalance. Cooperation, on the other hand, indicates that the parties involved are working together on the same team and share a common goal. Operating from a cooperative mindset naturally encourages cohesion, collaboration, and focus on harmony. To focus on cooperation, staff are encouraged to look for commonalities between their goals and the customer's wants. For example, *"The goal is to get you out of here and home to your family. Let's get you through all your (paperwork/tests/procedures) and get you moving toward that goal."* Staff can also encourage customers to help them make decisions together, demonstrating a desire to work together, and valuing the customer as a valued member of the team.

In situations where customers are reluctant to cooperate and collaborate, staff are encouraged to look for opportunities where the customer and staff can agree. Getting a "yes" response, even on something simple and unrelated (e.g., Can I get you a chair? Cup of water?), creates a cooperative exchange that can open the door for further agreement to other requests, as the customer starts viewing the staff as having something to offer them. Creating positive associations between the customer and staff can prevent aggression from forming, by a cooperating team mentality, and will help prevent and mitigate escalation.

Even when setting boundaries, it is important to approach this as a collaborative process, rather than an assertion of power or authority. One best practice is to consider establishing a formal outline of behavioral expectations with a customer, especially when the exhibited behaviors are concerning or repetitive. This outline is essentially a "contract" that defines plans for cooperative behaviors between the organization and the customer. This contract should focus on collaborations rather than ultimatums for the customer. Naming these contracts **"partnership agreements"** is a more positive term that lists how the organization and customer are mutually entering into an agreement to benefit both parties in getting their needs met. These written agreements should outline expectations for both parties involved, and, when followed, will allow for the relationship to be positive and violence free (e.g., *As a customer I agree to … As an organization we agree to …*). Holding both sides responsible for upholding expectations maintains a unified approach to a common goal, a safe environment for all involved. Again, remember to use soft language when preparing partnership agreements, as this will help customers be more receptive to cooperation.

When Things Escalate

In business there is a saying, "The customer is always right." Businesses often utilize this approach recognizing that in order for a business to operate, it needs its customers to keep coming back. Happy customers equal repeat customers and thriving business. Sometimes this results in businesses accommodating customers by making exceptions and focusing on customer satisfaction at the expense of the staff or business itself. But what happens when the customer is actually wrong? Or when the customer's negative actions (aggression and violence) are causing an unsafe environment? Is the customer still right?

Finding the balance between customer service and staff support is a tricky subject. Letting the customer always be right can result in frustration and agitation of the staff who are trying to enforce policies and workflows of the organization. This is especially true when staff attempt to enforce a policy and the customer requests to "speak to the manager." If the higher authority does not uphold the frontline staff's ruling, they run the risk of leaving staff feeling undermined, further frustrated, and being seen as "the bad guy" in the eyes of the customer. If this happens repeatedly, staff may feel helpless in these power struggles and either stop enforcing policies or leave the organization due to feeling powerless and dissatisfied as an employee. However, if the higher authority holds strong supporting the frontline staff, the customer may leave dissatisfied, opting to no longer utilize the business, possibly sharing their frustrations with others, which could hurt the reputation of the organization, costing it additional customers. Neither situation is ideal.

Making Exceptions

Rules exist for a reason. Policies and rules bring certainty and order to an organization so that everyone is operating from the same perspective on how things are expected to go. When exceptions are made, a gray zone is opened in which the rules do not always apply. Exceptions can, therefore, be a slippery slope, which if not considered carefully can result in the entire rule book getting thrown out, leading to confusion, disorganization, and aggression. However, it is also important to recognize that people make mistakes or misunderstand directions, and sometimes the rules need to be bent, given the specific circumstances. Making exceptions can often de-escalate an aggressive situation and repair relationships with a customer, without undermining the staff, if done wisely. Here are some things to consider when making exceptions.

First-Time Request for Exceptions

When considering making an exception (Figure 8.3), it is helpful to know whether this is a first-time occurrence or if the individual frequently bends or breaks the rules. If it is a first-time situation, truly seems to be a result of a miscommunication, and is feasible for an exception to be made, clearly communicate why the exception is granted and how the customer is expected to behave in future encounters.

Scenario: Building from the previous example:

Staff response: *"I'm sorry for the confusion. Here is the flyer with the current visitor guidelines that was just updated on Monday. It states that the visiting hours are from 12 pm to 4 pm today. I'm sure this must be frustrating as you thought you would have more time with your loved one. I know you only had 30 minutes to visit today, and I am willing to make an exception for you and allow you to stay until 5 pm today. Moving forward, you will need to visit within the visitation guidelines. You can take this flyer with you to have the visiting schedule as reference for your next visit."*

Figure 8.3: Example of Making an Exception

Extenuating Circumstances

Sometimes the situations we are confronted with are difficult to plan for and need to be reconsidered for special circumstances. While rules are needed for an organization to run smoothly, it is always important to remember that businesses exist for servicing people in our communities. Upholding policies for the sake of "rules are rules" misses the point that the business is about providing a service to people, and that people have feelings and needs too. If we lose the humanness behind the service our businesses provide, we lose what makes the organization meaningful at its core—helping people. Thinking about the situation from the customer's perspective and experience is important in staying connected to the humanness behind the work.

When it is appropriate to make exceptions based on extenuating circumstances that will change the rules/policies for a customer, it is important that this exception is clearly communicated to everyone that would be interacting with this individual AND that the exception is well-documented in an easily accessible place to be referenced in case there is any question about the details of the approved exception.

Empowering Staff

When a customer wants an exception to be made, they often ask to speak to someone of authority. One way to avoid this power struggle from happening is to empower your direct line staff to use their critical thinking skills to consider if an exception is appropriate before the customer asks to talk to the authority figure. By proactively identifying a potential for conflict, staff can begin to prepare for how to handle situations where exceptions might be requested or granted. If this is something that the staff needs to clear with an authority first, they can identify the customer's request and take the suggested exception to the authority for approval (Figure 8.4). By identifying the compromise or exception themselves, staff can align with the customer. The authority can still determine that the rule needs to be in place, but the staff member is less likely to experience aggression escalating to violence toward them, because the customer views the staff member as an advocate.

Scenario: Building from the previous example:

Staff response: *"I'm sorry for the confusion. Here is the flyer with the current visitor guidelines that was just updated on Monday. It states that the visiting hours are from 12 pm to 4 pm today. I'm sure this must be frustrating as you thought you would have more time with your loved one. I know you only had 30 minutes to visit today. Let me see if we can make an exception for you today. I'm going to talk to my supervisor. I'll be back in just a moment after we've had a chance to talk."*

Figure 8.4: Example of Empowered Staff Making Exceptions

Making Exceptions without Undermining Staff

When a supervisor, manager, or other person in an authority position is called in to make a ruling, they must be careful to balance customer service and staff support. This is particularly sensitive when the authority decides to grant an exception in a situation when the staff member believes the policy should be upheld or has already said "no" to an exception. As the deciding leader, it is important to take time to listen to the staff member's perspective and decision-making. Neglecting to listen to and consider the staff perspective will always result in a frustrated and hurt staff member who feels undermined. Even if the leader disagrees with the staff member, this is an opportunity to teach the staff about when to consider making exceptions and why exceptions sometimes need to be granted. Reviewing these situations with staff can empower them to know how to handle these types of situations in the future, without the need for a supervisor to get involved. When a staff member's decision is being overturned, it is helpful to let the staff member share the exception directly with the customer or be present beside the leader during that conversation. This prevents the appearance that the staff does not have a say and keeps them involved in the decision-making process. It also sends a message to the customer that they cannot just bypass the staff member as it demonstrates collaboration between the staff and leadership teams (Figure 8.5).

Scenario: Building from the previous example: Staff member decided to uphold visitation hours from 12 pm to 4 pm; customer asked to talk to manager.

Staff response: *"I spoke to my supervisor about your situation. I explained the confusion about the visitation policy today and that I clarified with you the current visitation policy. We decided that today we will grant you an exception to the policy and allow you to stay until 5 pm. Moving forward you will need to visit within the regular visitation hours. You can take this flyer with you to have the visiting schedule as reference for your future visits."*

Leader response: (With staff member present) *Thank you for taking the time to explain your request to me. My staff shared with me that they did inform you of the current visitation policy that will need to be followed moving forward. After further consideration, we both agreed to make an exception for you today as it seems you were unaware of the schedule. Today we will allow you to stay until 5 pm to give you some more time with your loved one. Moving forward you will need to visit within the regular visitation hours. You can take this flyer with you to have the visiting schedule as reference for your future visits."*

Figure 8.5: Example of Exception without Undermining Staff

When Violence Occurs: Restoring Safety

Unfortunately, even in organizations with strong prevention and intervention plans, situations of violence can occur. Therefore, it is imperative to establish initiatives to support staff when situations of aggression and violence impact the organization. Having a clear process for reporting, follow-up, emotional support, and education provides security and reassurance after WPV disrupts safety.

Reporting/Documentation

Every organization should have a system in place for staff to report situations of WPV and staff should be well-educated on how to report experiences. Documentation should be confidential in nature, without ramifications for reporting. Having a system in place lets staff know that the organization cares about their safety and wants to know when things are unsafe. (For more information on best practices for reporting and documenting, refer to Chapter 4.)

Leadership Follow-Up

Perhaps even more important than a place to document situations of WPV is the follow-up that the staff receive after a situation of violence occurs. After an act of violence occurs, it is imperative that the direct supervisor reaches out to their staff member within the first 24 hours or immediately upon learning about the situation. It is best practice that this follow-up communication occurs either in person or by spoken communication. It is not advised to conduct follow-up on workplace injury via e-mail or text as these are casual and impersonal ways of reaching out to show care and concern. Initial communication with the injured staff member should focus on the staff member's well-being as the paramount concern and not the logistics of what happened. While logistics are important, if injury has occurred, play-by-play of the interaction should be discussed at a later date.

Depending on the severity of the violence, the manager or supervisor should plan to check-in again with the staff member within the week after the incident. This additional check-in is advised because some individuals are still in shock and have not yet processed the violation of safety immediately following the violent interaction. A second check-in during the week after the event allows for the individual to move beyond any initial traumatic reactions and gives them time to process and reflect, making this a good time to discuss logistics and problem-solving. The manager or supervisor can assess if there is need for any additional emotional support and can refer the staff member to emotional support resources that the organization provides. Even if the staff member seems to be doing well, it is recommended that the manager or supervisor be mindful of any behavioral changes that may occur for the staff over the next month. Sometimes after incidents of violence individuals struggle to acknowledge the impact it has had on them or try to hide the emotional toll in efforts to "be strong." When this occurs, staff can start revealing they are struggling emotionally through uncharacteristic behaviors (e.g., tardiness, snapping at others, isolation, sudden decline in performance). Because these behaviors show up many weeks after the incident of violence, leaders sometimes neglect to consider that these problems may be related to recent traumatic experiences with WPV.

Staff Emotional Support

Having emotional support resources for staff following situations of WPV allows for emotional healing and increased resiliency. While many organizations have **employee assistance programs (EAPs)** that will connect staff to counseling services, it is becoming a best practice for organizations to have their own emotional support staff whose role is providing confidential individual and group intervention through supportive listening, consultation, mental health education, mental health referral, crisis debriefing, and decompression. Having an on-site emotional support coordinator shows the organization's commitment to employee mental well-being and allows for staff to be able to access resources for stress and emotional distress in its infancy. By addressing stressors early, staff can build resiliency tools and get connected to supportive resources before they are unable to work and need to take time off. It also means that staff can decompress from stressors in the moment, helping to prevent the buildup of frustrations and decreasing the chances of stress impacting their future customer interactions. When staff can decompress safely in a therapeutic and appropriate way, they are less likely to take stress out on customers, and WPV/aggression decreases.

WPV Debriefings

Another best practice for WPV is to hold confidential **Critical Incident Stress Debriefings (CISD)** for emotional processing and support for anyone impacted by the situation. An **emotional debriefing** is an opportunity shortly after a situation of violence that allows those involved to process the emotional impact of the violence. Holding a debriefing can help a traumatized individual or group regain a sense of stability and cohesion after violence strikes, with the added benefit of reducing the chances that the impacted individuals develop longer lasting traumatic reactions (2). In addition to being able to process the emotional reaction, which serves to lower emotional tension, a debrief helps the individuals involved to identify their healthy coping strategies and existing supports and connects them to additional resources as needed. (For additional information on debriefs, refer to Chapter 3.) For more information on CISD, please refer to the International Critical Incident Stress Foundation, Inc.

Annual Training and Education

In order for staff to be able to handle situations of escalating aggression and violence, it is critical that they receive adequate training. While many organizations focus on staff education at the hiring and onboarding stages of employment, it is highly recommended that training be repeated to keep information in immediate recall and current with the best practice standards. WPV education should include both aspects of awareness and psychoeducation, as well as practical application of de-escalation strategies/interventions. Education on intervention strategies should match the customer population and potential risk interactions. Additionally, it is important when discussing WPV to remember that situations of aggression and violence are not isolated to customer/staff interactions. Education should incorporate examples of WPV with a wide variety of scenarios including customer-to-staff violence, staff-to-customer violence, customer-to-customer violence, and staff-to-staff violence (Figure 8.6).

Topics for Psychoeducation on Prevention:
- Sexual harassment
- Discrimination (including gender, race, ethnicity, culture, disability, sexual preference, age, religion)
- Unconscious bias
- Microaggressions
- Gender identity
- Trauma-informed care
- Risk assessment
- Policies on workplace violence (including how to report)
- Resources available to staff (e.g., EAP, **VESSA Leave**)

Practical Intervention Education:
- Verbal de-escalation
- Disengagement techniques
- Physical intervention techniques
- Active threat trainingPlease treat the staff with the same respect you would expect to receive.

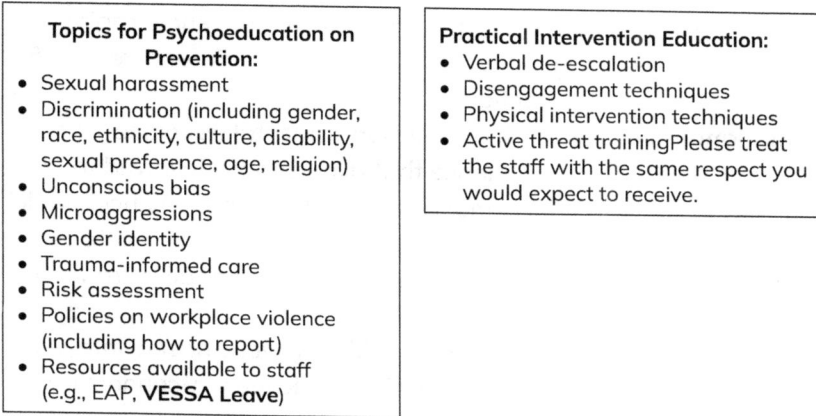

Figure 8.6: Education Topics for Staff for Psychoeducation and Intervention

References

1. Mehrabian, A. 1971. *Silent Messages: Implicit Communication of Emotions and Attitudes.* 1st ed. Belmont, CA: Wadsworth Publishing Company. ISBN: 0534000592.
2. Mitchell, J.T. 2017. *Group Crisis Intervention.* Ellicott City, MD: International Critical Incident Stress Foundation, Inc. ISBN: 978-0-9795692-0-3.

Glossary of Terms

Behavior Contract A written document outlining expectations for an individual's behavior and the likely consequences for failing to uphold those expectations.

Critical Incident Stress Debriefing (CISD) a specific, 7-step process where a supportive, crisis-focused discussion is facilitated with a small, homogeneous group of people who encountered a powerful traumatic event. It aims at reduction of distress and a restoration of group cohesion and unit performance.

Culture of Safety Signage Marketing materials used by an organization to communicate the organization's stance on violence being unacceptable in the workplace and encouraging an atmosphere of healthy boundaries, and safe and respectful interpersonal interactions.

Emotional Debriefing A discussion that takes place shortly after a situation of violence that allows those involved to process and share the emotional impact of the violence, while also identifying coping skills and strategies to promote resiliency and decrease the chances of long-standing traumatic responses.

Employee Assistance Program (EAP) A work-based intervention program designed to assist employees in connecting to resources to help resolve personal stressors.

Mirroring A nonverbal form of active listening in which the listener reflects the affect and body language of the speaker in order to convey a sense of empathy and understanding.

Nonverbal Communication The message conveyed in conversation through facial expressions, gestures, tone of voice, volume of voice, body language, physical proximity, eye contact, appearance, etc.

Paraverbal Communication The parts of verbal communication beyond the words being spoken, including volume, pace (speed), rhythm, tone, pitch that contributes to the message being conveyed.

Partnership Agreement A written document outlining expectations for an individual's behavior and the likely consequences for failing to uphold those expectations.

Soft language The use of a gentle tone of voice that is understanding, compassionate, and supportive.

VESSA Leave Victims' Economic Security and Safety Act (VESSA) allows employees who are victims of violence to take up to 12 weeks of unpaid leave for any 12-month period to seek medical help and legal assistance.

Workplace Violence (WPV) Any act or threat of physical violence, harassment, intimidation, or other threatening disruptive behavior that occurs at the work site.

CHAPTER 9

Workplace Violence in the Ambulatory and Alternate Care Sites

Kimberly A. Urbanek and Laura Larkin

Objectives

After reading this chapter, one should be able to:

- Understand the growing trends of violence and common triggers in ambulatory and alternate care sites (AACS)
- Identify the seven steps of establishing a workplace violence prevention (WPVP) program specific to the AACS
- Create a workplace violence (WPV) committee specific to the AACS
- Identify challenges and barriers of a WPV program in AACS
- Develop and implement WPVP initiatives and solutions in the AACS

When thinking about **workplace violence (WPV)** in health care, all eyes typically turn toward hospitals. It is well known that emergency departments, behavioral health units, and critical care units are high-risk areas for violence and escalation. Due to the patient population and the high number of incidents in these departments, it is easy to see why these areas become a priority. However, there is a less obvious worry that needs to be seen, and that is the growing problem with WPV in the **ambulatory and alternate care sites (AACS)**. Ambulatory care sites are areas where care is provided by health care professionals in outpatient settings, away from the hospital. Examples of ambulatory care sites include physician offices, health clinics, immediate cares, physical rehabilitation centers, ambulatory surgery centers, dental offices, diagnostic imaging centers, home health, hospice, and dialysis centers. Alternate care sites are areas where residential care can be provided by health care professionals, but in locations outside of the hospital. Care in these areas may be short term, as they are in skilled nursing facilities or rehabilitation centers, or long term, as they are in nursing homes or assisted living facilities.

WPV in the AACS is a long-standing issue, but for various reasons has not traditionally been a focus for health care organizations. Resources are often allocated to the development of a prevention program in the main hospitals, with the issues in AACS left largely unattended. However, this is a mistake. Hospitals may seem larger in scope and practice, but patient visits in the AACS make up a large percentage of a hospital's overall revenue. Recent studies have shown that the "aggregate outpatient share of total hospital revenue grew from 28 percent in 1994 to 48 percent in 2018" and is still growing each year (1). As health care is shifting to provide care in less costly, more convenient ways, the growth of outpatient settings is an integral part of the future of health care. The number of employees at these sites is growing and rivals the number of employees that make up the hospital staff. Furthermore, the number of patient visits in the AACS far surpasses the number of patient visits in the hospital setting. In fact, patients spend a majority of their time receiving care in outpatient settings, working to manage chronic conditions and prevent hospital admissions. In 2018, there were over 860.4 million office visits in the ambulatory care setting, which grew to approximately 900.6 million in 2019 (2). In comparison, there were only 36.2 million hospital admissions in 2019 (3). Figures 9.1 and 9.2 demonstrate how inpatient and outpatient hospital revenue are converging when looking at overall revenue. In addition, one-third of all mental health care provided in the United States is being treated by primary care **providers** in ambulatory office settings, (4). "Twenty four percent of those patients have a diagnosed mental health disorder," which may increase the risk for violence (4). These numbers demonstrate the growing populations that are passing through the doors of the AACS every day. According to an executive brief issued by the Emergency Care Research Institute (ECRI) Patient Safety Organization (PSO) in 2019, WPV is one of the top four key risks in ambulatory care settings (5). Therefore, while a considerable amount of time, effort, and money are often focused on hospital violence prevention, it is vital to include AACS in the development of **workplace violence prevention (WPVP)** programs. AACS can no longer be excluded.

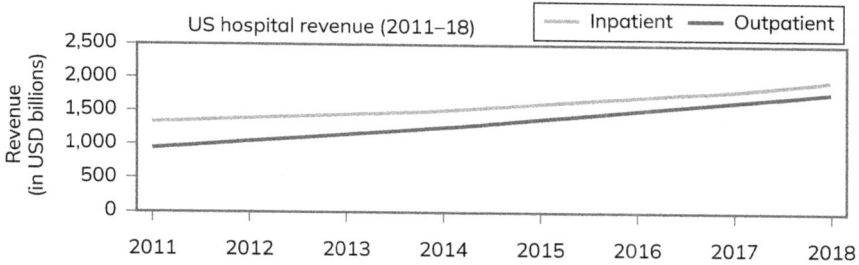

Figure 9.1: Total Revenue from Inpatient and AACS (6)

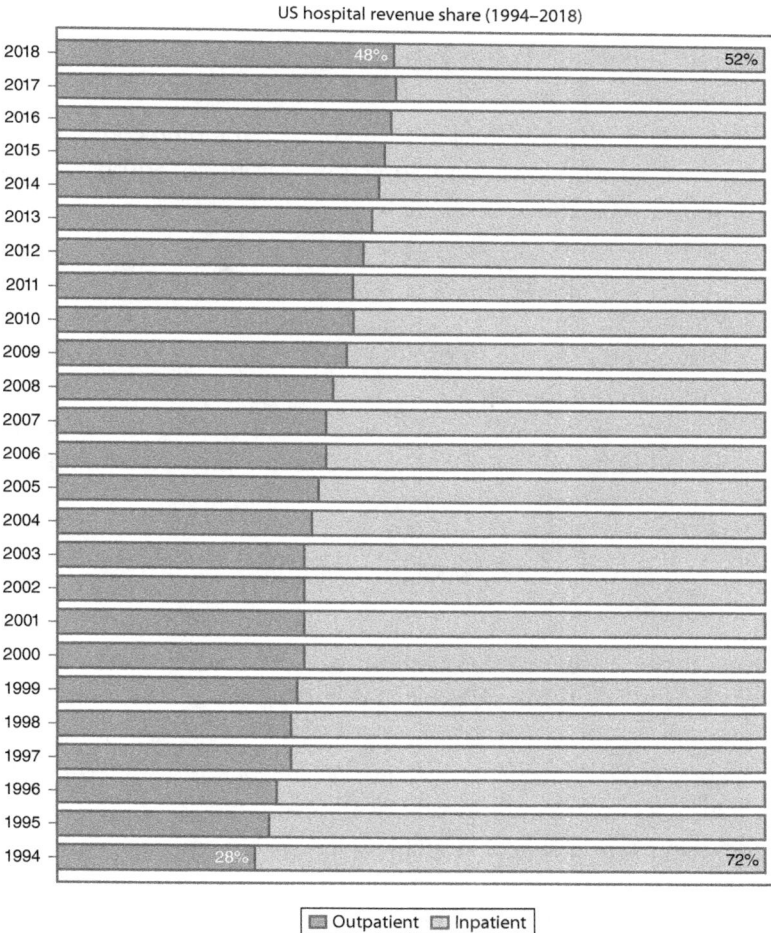

Figure 9.2: Outpatient Services Growth (1)

Violence in the AACS

Type 2 violence, or violence perpetrated by patients and visitors, is the most common type of violence that occurs in the ambulatory and alternate care settings. (See Chapter 6 for more info on the four types of violence.) Staff in these settings can experience rampant incidents of verbal assault and abuse. These incidents may include verbal aggression, threats, acts of intimidation, harassment, bullying, and sabotage (7). On occasion, these verbal incidents can escalate and develop into physical incidents and may even result in workplace injuries. There are some consistent topics that can make caring for patients difficult in the AACS when they surface. Below are some common themes that are often the cause of escalation:

- Chronic pain
- Impaired cognitive ability (dementia, Alzheimer, confusion, etc.)
- Impaired ability to communicate (language barriers, hard of hearing, slurred speech, etc.)
- Scheduling/accessibility issues
- Finance/billing issues
- Wait times
- Disagreement with treatment plans
- Drug-seeking behaviors
- Disagreement with office policies (appointment rescheduling, tardiness for appointments, prescription refill requirements, etc.)
- Untreated mental health/psychiatric conditions
- Unmet/unreasonable expectations
- Difficult family members/family matters
- Addictions

These topics of concern are familiar to anyone working in AACS. Staff and providers deal with upset individuals daily and need to have the tools to manage these behaviors appropriately. The prevalence of these incidents clearly outlines the strong need for violence prevention practices in the AACS. Knowing how to address these topics and having a plan for when they arise is critical to building a safe, violent-free environment. Proactively training staff on these areas allows sites to better manage escalation when staff recognize these patterns and respond appropriately.

Establishing a WPV Program in the AACS

Establishing a WPV program in the ambulatory sites is not as daunting as it may seem. Even small steps in the right direction can go a long way in these areas. In addition, there are usually existing pieces of a program that can be extended to the AACS. It just takes a little attention and creativity to develop a successful and robust program in these settings. Below are seven steps to consider when growing the WPV program at the AACS (Figure 9.3).

7 Steps of WPV at Ambulatory and Alternate Care Sites

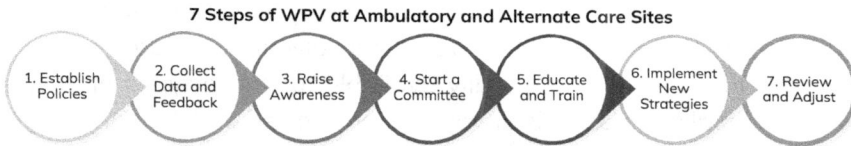

1. Establish Policies
2. Collect Data and Feedback
3. Raise Awareness
4. Start a Committee
5. Educate and Train
6. Implement New Strategies
7. Review and Adjust

Figure 9.3: Seven Steps to WPVP in the AACS

Seven Steps of WPVP for the AACS

Step 1: Build the Foundation

The first step toward establishing a WPV program in the AACS is to learn what is already in place within the organization. Learn what the current WPV policy says. Is it specific to hospital staff or inclusive of staff in all locations? Is there an active WPV committee that meets regularly? Is there someone from the AACS on the committee? Having the voice of AACS in these committees and policies is essential. Having AACS leadership contribute to the organization's overall program and policy development will be integral to building awareness about issues in those sites. AACS leaders need to play an active role on the inpatient WPV committee and represent their areas in the planning. This involvement aligns the AACS goals with the organization's strategic goals. This involvement also affords connections to strategic partners such as public safety, risk management, nursing, and physician leaders. It is also a venue to learn about current successful hospital initiatives, practices, and strategies that can be implemented and adapted to the AACS. If an alternate site is not directly connected to a hospital, it will be important to establish a WPV policy for these stand-alone locations. There are several credible resources with guidelines on what to include in a WPV policy, such as the **Occupational Safety and Health Administration (OSHA)**, the **International Association of Health Care Security and Safety (IAHSS)**, and the **Canadian Center of Occupational Health and Safety (CCOHS)**.

Step 2: Learn the Current Climate

The next step is data collection and analysis. Is there existing data being captured specific to WPV in the ambulatory and alternate settings? Most incidents that occur in these sites involve verbal aggression, so incident data may not be readily available for these types of occurrences. Verbal aggression is always underreported and if reporting has not previously been emphasized with staff, it can be difficult to get a feel for the pulse of what is happening at these sites. If statistics do already exist, it can be helpful, but total number of incidents may not be enough. It is important to determine the details about what degree of verbal abuse is occurring. Is staff experiencing rudeness, yelling, name calling, belittling, or threats? Are these different categories being captured? Staff would be expected to respond differently to each of these incidents. There might be an expectation to just ignore rudeness and not take it personally. Instead, staff should empathize with the patient. However, if someone was directly threatening staff, there would be an expectation for staff to move to safety and seek assistance. All threats should be taken seriously and investigated, which is a different expectation in staff response. To establish expectations and train staff how to safely respond, there is a need to understand what types of events are occurring.

Of course, physical injury data is also important to review. Fortunately, physical injuries are not as prevalent in the AACS as they are in the inpatient setting. However, it is important to determine if there is still a degree of physical aggression or abuse occurring. These incidents look different in the AACS. Physically aggressive incidents can involve slamming a door, throwing a pen, pushing past someone, swatting at someone, etc. These incidents are not as obvious or severe as punching or kicking, so they are sometimes overlooked. These expressions of physical aggression tend to be more common in the AACS and can be precursors to additional violence where staff should have heightened awareness. Below are data points that should be collected to track incidents in the AACS to determine where the greatest risk exists (Table 9.1).

Table 9.1: Data to Track for Ambulatory and Alternate Care Sites

Date of Incident
Time of Incident
Building/Location of Incident
Department/Unit Where Incident Occurred
Offender Name
Offender Type (Patient/Visitor/Student/Staff/Provider/etc.)
Offender Gender
Offender Age
Summary of Event
Victim(s) Name
Victim(s) Type (Patient/Visitor/Student/Staff/Provider/etc.)
Victim Job Title (Nurse/Technician/Public/Safety/Mental Health/Registration/Other, etc.)
Verbal Event (Yes/No)
Type of Verbal Event: • Anxiety • Challenging/Untrusting • Refusal/Uncooperative • Yelling/Screaming • Threatening
Physical Contact (Yes/No)
Any injuries? (Yes/No)
Injury Data (Location of Injury, Mechanism of Injury)
Is it a reportable incident? (OSHA Reportable/Sentinel Event?)
Any lost work days/modified duty?

If reliable statistics are not available, another way to procure information quickly is through staff feedback. Since the topic of WPV may be untapped in these settings, staff are likely to share a lot of information if asked. **Rounding** is a great way to get immediate feedback and see how the morale of staff is affected by incidents. A WPV survey may be another way to quickly determine how staff are feeling about their safety in the workplace. When rounding or surveying staff, some questions that should be asked are:

- Do you often encounter verbal or physical aggression?
- Have you ever experienced WPV that you did not report? If so, why?
- Do you feel you have the necessary training to handle verbal/physical aggression?
- Do you feel supported when facing verbal/physical aggression?
- Does your supervisor emphasize workplace safety?
- Does the organization focus on safety of the workforce?
- Does the organization focus on safety of the patients?
- Do you feel the organization does everything it can to keep you safe?

The above questions allow an opportunity to get some feedback on the staff, management, and the organization. Look for trends and patterns to begin to address deficiencies. It is also important to listen to the staff stories. There are plenty of pain points that can surface when you listen for the underlying details. What themes are you hearing? Where are staff having the most difficulties? Is it with scheduling? Family members? Is there a clunky process that continues to cause upsets? What is one thing that staff KNOW always upsets people? Start there. Identify at least one area that can be the first "project." Identify a well-known pain point and make it a priority to address. If that pain point is too large of a lift to start with, pick a smaller pain point for a quick win. Any attention that is focused on issues that staff have called out will surely be a benefit. Share key data and findings with senior leaders and important stakeholders in the organization to raise awareness. Uncovering issues and concerns that exist in these sites opens the door to improved safety in these locations. Establishing the need and garnering support from senior leaders and AACS management will be essential to the development of the WPVP program in the AACS.

Step 3: Start a Campaign

Once a policy has been established and challenges have been identified, start a campaign about the importance of WPVP. Begin to raise awareness about the goal of addressing violence and aggression. Create opportunities to be loud and visible about the focus on improving the situation. Staff will begin to feel heard and valued. The issues that they silently tolerate every day are finally being recognized and addressed. Communicate about WPV awareness regularly. Drive staff to report incidents so more information can be discovered. Share safety stories about situations that occurred and use them as learning opportunities across your sites. Shout successes from the rooftops so that it becomes obvious to staff how committed the organization is to supporting them and encouraging their safety. There are usually many initiatives that are happening behind the scenes that may impact WPV so bring those to the forefront. Continue to round and be visible to staff so they see signs of commitment to this issue. Being visible and transparent in all these ways helps rebuild some of the trust that may have eroded a bit, as well as helps keep management teams accountable. Every employee should be able to speak to the work being done to further WPVP in the organization, at every level.

Step 4: Find Your People

Once there is a buzz about what the organization is working to accomplish for the benefit of staff at the AACS, there will be some people who surface that are interested and engaged. Look for these people. Make it a movement. Empower staff to have a voice about safety in their environments. Create a WPV committee specifically for the AACS as a best practice. This committee can be a separate, stand-alone committee, or a subcommittee that reports up through the inpatient WPV committee.

Be sure to include key players. Committee members should be a diverse enough group to be representative of frontline staff, supervisory staff, providers, nurses, and other disciplines that exist within the building(s). Include representation from diagnostic hospital departments and support areas that share space in these locations (lab, imaging, rehab, registration, etc.). Ensure that a senior leader is involved. Recruit a respected physician to sit on the committee so they can champion the issues to other providers. There may be a need to involve some inpatient area representatives on this committee as well, such as Public Safety, Risk Management, Occupational Health and Safety staff, etc. (Table 9.2).

Table 9.2: Common Roles and Areas That Should Be Represented on the AACS Committee

Roles to Consider:
Senior Leader of Ambulatory Services
Manager/Director of Quality or Compliance
Patient Experience Representative/Patient Advocate
Clinical Educators
Nursing Managers/Nursing Supervisors
Manager/Supervisor of Registration Services
Physician
Nurse
Medical Assistant/Patient Care Technician
Behavioral Health Clinician
Manager of Greeters/Concierge
Manager of Public Safety
Risk Management for Ambulatory sites

Additional Areas to Include as Needed:
Lab/Phlebotomy
Imaging Services (X-ray, CT, MRI, Mammography, etc.)
Neurology/Pain Clinics
Rehabilitation Services
Behavioral Health Outpatient Services
Diabetes Services
Weight Loss Clinic
Outpatient Surgery Centers
Family Medicine (FM)/Internal Medicine (IM)
Obstetrics (OB)/Gynecology (GYN)
Pediatrics
Medical Subspecialties (Allergy, Endocrinology, Rheumatology, etc.)
Surgical Subspecialties (Ears/Nose/Throat (ENT), Gastroenterology, Ortho, etc.)

The leader(s) for the ambulatory WPV committee will need to determine the logistics of the committee. There will be several questions that need to be answered initially. What topics should be regularly included on the agendas? How frequently should the team meet? What time of day is best for full attendance at committee meetings? Who will chair the committee and what senior leader will sponsor? Key topics for AACS WPV committee meetings can include:

- Communication and awareness of WPV
- Physical assessment of workspaces
- Training plans and training needs (initial and ongoing)
- How to handle escalation/practical applications
- Review of significant issues and high-risk areas
- Review of incident and injury data and new trends/concerns
- New ideas/initiatives
- Weapons in the workplace

Step 5: Education

A fundamental training need for AACS staff is training on de-escalation and limit setting. Of course, staff will benefit from learning many other topics, but starting with de-escalation and limit setting can make the biggest impact. Staff should understand that they are part of a chain of interactions and being observant of potentially escalating patient behaviors allows them to proactively respond and resolve concerns. Staff can address behaviors early, so they do not escalate during later interactions. For example, staff may see someone who is anxious and pacing, and unable to sit in the waiting room. Instead of considering it a normal and common event that they often witness, staff should recognize this as a warning sign and should provide a supportive, calm response, which will likely improve how the next interaction will go. Staff typically want to learn how to better manage crisis situations. By giving them the tools and permission to de-escalate and set limits, staff are empowered and better equipped to understand that everyone owns a piece of the patient experience. Creating a culture where these behaviors are practiced daily by staff will begin to establish consistent expectations for AACS patients and customers. Putting these techniques into practice can quite literally change the climate of their environment.

Often, organizations purchase a violence prevention education program. This program can be used to train staff with the skills needed to safely recognize and respond to everyday scenarios that arise in health care. Be sure that the program is applicable to the AACS settings. A relevant program can provide an excellent framework for de-escalation and limit setting, which are most often needed in the ambulatory setting. In place of a purchased program, specific education can be created for the AACS without any additional cost. Education can be created by the AACS WPV committee as a project or can involve a group of interested staff to assist. Some education initiatives that can be employed when educating on prevention are:

- Record a video showing a common situation of verbal aggression. Engage key staff members to role-play. Do one version showing the "wrong" way to respond, and one version showing the "right" way to de-escalate. Videos can be reviewed briefly at department meetings or shift changes or can be placed on the organization's learning platform to be distributed to staff to complete at a time that's best for them.
- Utilize actual reported incidents and conduct a debrief to learn more details and guide staff on other possible solutions. Reviewing camera footage of actual incidents can also prove to be educational, if available.
- Share a story of a time staff successfully managed verbal aggression. Celebrate the skills that were utilized during de-escalation. This story can be shared at shift change or via e-mail or a communication board, etc.
- Conduct a live action scenario before the office opens for the day. Have a staff member play the role of the patient and other staff rotate through the de-escalation role. This allows staff to gain some experience in a "safe" environment and reflect on ways to improve their response.
- Create scripting or "conversation starters" for common situations where staff experience refusal or push back. Rehearsing these phrases allows staff to build "muscle memory" and confidence in delivering the message. Staff can create a mental library of "go-to" messages, so they do not have to think up appropriate wording in the moment.

The above education approaches can be used as opportunities to engage AACS staff. They know their areas best and will be great contributors to the development of the program. Having staff directly participate in the creation of the prevention program immediately enhances ownership and empowers staff. As stated by Benjamin Franklin, "Tell me and I forget, teach me and I may remember, involve me and I learn."

Step 6: Prevention in Action

Work toward implementing WPVP initiatives that are specific to the AACS locations. Pick a couple of projects that can be started and get staff involved. These WPVP projects can be initiatives for the ambulatory WPV committee to work on or can be the responsibility of smaller teams or project groups that can report up to the committee. Use project charters as a tool for tracking progress of improvement teams. A charter creates a clear vision for the project. Align projects with goals that were developed by the AACS WPV committee. Reporting status updates on progress holds teams accountable for completion of action items. Discover other initiatives in the organization that could be adapted to the AACS. For example, most hospitals have an **Internal Response Team (IRT)** or a behavioral response team that can be activated for escalating situations, where a team of peers responds to assist and support with de-escalation. This initiative is a best practice and should be adapted and implemented in all AACS settings. Staff could activate this response by announcing a predetermined code word to alert teammates to the need for assistance with an escalating patient. Some proven examples of code words that can be used discreetly to request assistance are BERT (Behavioral Emergency Response Team) or ART (Ambulatory Response Team). Staff could simply call out, "Can BERT please come to the front desk" or "Send ART to exam Room 7." Code words can be determined based on what works for each organization, but needs to be consistent between all sites. (For more information on IRTs, refer to AACS key initiatives later in this chapter, or refer to Chapter 3.)

Step 7: Review

The effectiveness of the WPVP program can be monitored in different ways. Incidence and injury data can be used as a measure of performance improvement. Graphing this data monthly is ideal. Include annotation of when initiatives and education were completed and monitor for changes in trends. Determine how initiatives have affected overall incidents. For example, mark the graph timeline with the date that de-escalation education was completed and examine the results to observe the impact of the intervention (Figure 9.4). These data points and trends should be shared regularly at WPV committee meetings and with appropriate senior leaders to demonstrate the effectiveness of the WPVP training program. This data is also helpful when additional support or funding is needed to further prevention programs.

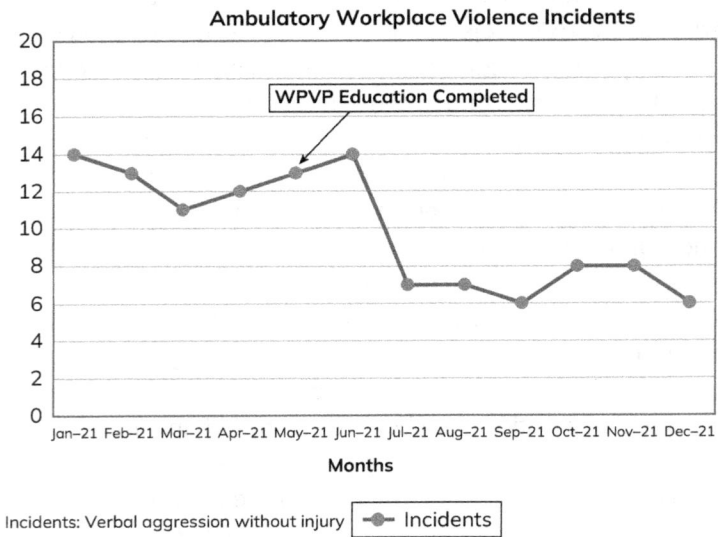

Ambulatory Workplace Violence Incidents

WPVP Education Completed

Months

Incidents: Verbal aggression without injury | Incidents

Figure 9.4: Graph Showing Total Number of Incidents and Impact of Prevention Initiatives

Follow-up surveys should be used as an additional measure of performance improvement. Numerous commercial surveys are available for purchase if an organization chooses to utilize a vendor for their surveys, rather than creating their own. If purchasing a survey service, evaluate the tool based on the ability to provide breakdown and analysis of the collected data. Consider sending surveys at least annually, to evaluate program effectiveness and impact in a timely manner. Be sure to use the same survey questions each time the survey is distributed, so that current results can be consistently compared to previous data. Survey data should also be shared with key stakeholders. Ongoing rounding on the unit continues to be an important source of feedback as well. After capturing statistical trends, reviewing feedback and survey results, and evaluating program progress, determine if the goals and priorities of the WPVP program need to be adjusted or not. By analyzing formal and informal outcomes, the team can further identify any new opportunities for improvement or may determine when additional education will be necessary. Continuous adjustments to the WPVP program will ensure safer environments in the AACS.

Key Initiatives to Implement in AACS

Just like in the hospitals, there are challenges in implementing a WPVP program in the AACS, although those challenges can look quite different. Below are some common obstacles that need to be considered when implementing WPVP strategies at AACS, along with some best practices for how to counter these concerns.

- *Challenge*: Building may be leased/not owned by the health care organization—no Public Safety presence; limits physical security measures (card readers, cameras, panic buttons, etc.); limits building-wide communication alerts.

  Solutions: Develop a do-it-yourself environmental security assessment for staff walkthroughs; conduct hazard assessments of space; create a plan for responding to violent incidents; identify where locks can be placed to restrict patient access from the front to the back of the office; create designated "safe spaces" for staff; identify a location near the front desk where an escalating patient in the waiting room can be moved to. This moves the danger away from other patients and removes the audience, which further tempers some patients; arrange furniture to prevent entrapment; a quick win can result from ensuring staff have clear access to exit the room; exam room tables should be placed furthest away from the exits.

- *Challenge*: Span of Control—AACS staff may float from site to site and managers may be responsible for multiple locations. This can make oversight and education more challenging. Staff unaware of specific building procedures/resources.

Solutions: Utilize the education methods listed above; assign training online or allow virtual meetings; establish same procedures across all entities; incorporate a representative on the AACS WPV committee from each building. Create "Safety Champions" at each location (at least one per floor) to assist with consistency.

- *Challenge*: Volume—number of patients that staff are exposed to each day is much higher than the inpatient setting; high number of patient encounters creates more opportunities for exposure to violence.

Solutions: Create a board or webpage for staff to reference with all of the staff resources; get staff trained in crisis prevention, mental health first aid, de-escalation, and limit setting. Create scripting for common scenarios; design reminder placards to place in discreet areas to prompt staff on de-escalation techniques (Figure 9.5). Communicate repeat offenders to the **Threat Assessment Team** (refer to Chapter 1 for more information on Threat Assessment Teams).

- *Challenge*: Mixed treatment teams—AACS teams work very closely with providers who are often unaware of any WPVP initiatives; some providers have more than one site where they practice; providers may unknowingly undermine staff as they may not experience the aggression that staff experience.

Solutions: Involve physicians on the WPV committee; include WPVP strategies and incident data on the agenda for physician leadership meetings. Create shortened training modules for providers and inform them of office initiatives so they can support staff. Find a respected physician to champion the initiatives and raise awareness among their peers. Inform physicians of WPVP goals and ensure expectation of safety is promoted and supported across all disciplines and levels of authority.

- *Challenge*: Isolated staff—departments in AACS have minimum staffing; may have only one employee in radiology or lab; staff in these areas are isolated and unaware of what may be occurring outside their own doors.

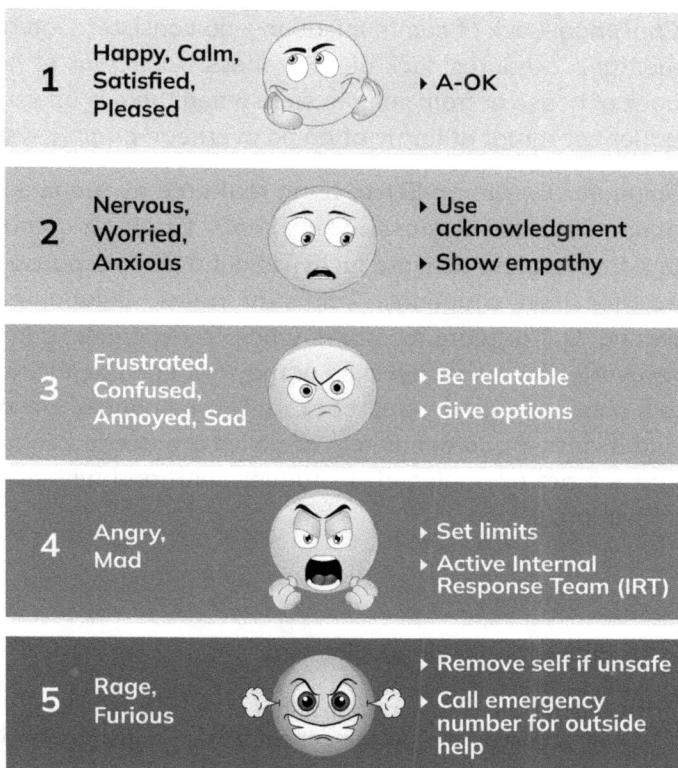

1	Happy, Calm, Satisfied, Pleased		▸ A-OK
2	Nervous, Worried, Anxious		▸ Use acknowledgment ▸ Show empathy
3	Frustrated, Confused, Annoyed, Sad		▸ Be relatable ▸ Give options
4	Angry, Mad		▸ Set limits ▸ Active Internal Response Team (IRT)
5	Rage, Furious		▸ Remove self if unsafe ▸ Call emergency number for outside help

Figure 9.5: De-escalation Prompts for Staff Based on Patient Presentation.
Note: Placards can be placed at front desk to remind staff which techniques to use when de-escalating

Kimberly A. Urbanek, Amanda Spagnolo, and Illustration created by Joan Wedge

Solutions: Consider quarterly "building" meetings to connect with other coworkers in different suites/departments; examine possible interdepartmental communication methods/alerts for incidents. Have department representation on the WPV committee. Create an IRT in all departments so that individual staff can have someone respond to support them in escalated situations. Implement mandatory team debriefings after each incident to look for improvement opportunities. (Refer to Chapter 3 for more information on debriefings.)

- *Challenge*: Lack of communication—no consistent interdepartmental procedures; lack of awareness from front of house to back of house or from suite to suite when there is an escalating patient or threat of harm; often no overhead paging system.

  Solutions: Create an IRT to bring real-time awareness to situations of verbal aggression or threats. Establish a code word and train staff to activate an IRT to get a peer response of support for these situations. Train staff in de-escalation and limit setting. Utilize team members who are experienced in service recovery. The responder may or may not need to intervene but is a show of support and backup. The responder will observe and assess if additional help or police are needed. Figures 9.6 and 9.7 are examples of a situation with and without an IRT activation.

Scenario #1: Patient is late for appointment

Patient arrives for his 3 pm doctor's appointment at 3:20 pm. The front desk staff member politely informs the patient that his appointment will need to be rescheduled since he is more than 15 min late, and there's strict office rules about being late. The patient begins screaming at the staff: "This is ridiculous! I have an appointment and need to see the doctor today! I got off of work early and raced over here. It's not my fault there was a damn accident in front of me. You're stupid if you think I'm rescheduling! I'm not leaving without being seen, so just do your damn job!" The staff member contacts the clinical team to let them know of patient's late arrival. The doctor decides he'll see the patient anyway and will just squeeze him in. The patient is taken to the exam room and the visit continues without further issues. Upon debriefing the incident staff concerns are revealed.

- Staff found it difficult to address the behavior as there were others in the waiting room.
- Staff felt intimidated and isolated since no other team members in the back were aware of what was happening.
- Doctor stated he would not have seen the patient had he known about the poor behavior.
- Staff felt unsupported and undermined while trying to enforce the office rules.

Figure 9.6: Verbal Aggression Scenario Without Any Support

<u>**Scenario #2: Patient is late for appointment and (Internal Response**</u>
<u>**Team) IRT activated**</u>

Patient arrives for his 3 pm doctor's appointment at 3:20 pm. The front desk staff member politely informs the patient that his appointment will need to be rescheduled since he is more than 15 min late, and there's strict office rules about being late. The patient begins screaming at the staff: "This is ridiculous! I have an appointment and need to see the doctor today! I got off of work early and raced over here. It's not my fault there was a damn accident in front of me. You're stupid if you think I'm rescheduling! I'm not leaving without being seen, so just do your damn job!"

Staff acknowledges patient concerns and validates feelings. "I'm sorry to hear you've had a hard time getting here today. That must be so frustrating." Staff member activates an IRT by using the code word. "Can Dr. IRT come up to the front please?" The alert can be vocal, via phone, page, or instant message. At least one other team member immediately responds to the front desk to assist and support the staff member. She stands next to the staff member and closely observes and intervenes as needed. Responding team member sets limits and asks patient to have a seat while they determine if anything can be done to accommodate him. Patient complies. Doctor is informed about the IRT. Doctor agrees to see the patient but addresses the behavior with the patient at the beginning of the visit. Doctor informs patient that this was a one-time exception made for the tardiness. Doctor also explains that the incivility and verbal abuse toward staff members is inappropriate and will not be tolerated. Patient informed that if behavior continues, he will not be able to continue as a patient at this clinic. Patient apologized to doctor, and later to staff, thanking them for their help. When debriefing the incident, it was revealed:

- Staff felt supported and empowered to respond appropriately
- Additional staff presence helped balance out the power struggle
- Staff learned additional methods/scripting to use when attempting to de-escalate
- Communication improved since all team members were aware of active situation
- Expectations were set with patient around future behaviors and documented
- Integrity of the staff/patient relationship remained intact

Figure 9.7: Verbal Aggression Scenario with IRT Activation

AACS no longer need to be left out of the discussion when it comes to WPV. In fact, as violent encounters continue to grow, organizations need to take a serious look to determine what types of incidents are occurring in their own locations, and how this is negatively impacting staff, providers, and patients. Organizations can make real strides in the reduction of WPV in their AACS just by focusing on and prioritizing some of the known issues. Implementation of the strategies outlined in this chapter have proven to be successful practices for an AACS and have yielded many positive benefits. Employees feel a sense of renewed safety and security when their de-escalations skills are enhanced, and they feel heard and supported by leadership. This provides for improvements in both staff morale and patient experience.

References

1. Abrams, Ken, Andreea Balan-Cohen, and Priyanshi Durbha. 2018. "Growth in Outpatient Care." *Deloitte Insights*, August 15, 2018. https://www2.deloitte.com/us/en/insights/industry/health-care/outpatient-hospital-services-medicare-incentives-value-quality.html.
2. The National Ambulatory Medical Care Survey (NAMCS). 2018. "National Ambulatory Medical Care Survey: 2018 National Summary Tables." *CDC.gov*, 2019. https://www.cdc.gov/nchs/data/ahcd/namcs_summary/2018-namcs-web-tables-508.pdf.
3. Michas, Frédéric. 2021. "Total Number of Hospital Admissions in the U.S. from 1946 to 2019." *Statista*, August 10, 2021. https://www.statista.com/statistics/459718/total-hospital-admission-number-in-the-us/.
4. Folgo, Ashley R., and Joanne DeSanto Iennaco. 2020. "Staff Perceptions of Risk Factors for Violence and Aggression in Ambulatory Care." *Work* 65 (2): 435–45. https://doi.org/10.3233/wor-203096.
5. ECRI. 2017. "Violence in Healthcare Facilities." *ECRI Institute*, May 24, 2017. https://www.ecri.org/components/HRC/Pages/SafSec3.aspx?PF=1%3Fsource.
6. Gerhardt, Wendy, and Ankit Arora. 2020. "Hospital Revenue Trends: Outpatient, Home Virtual, and Other Care Settings are Becoming More Common." *Deloitte Insights*, February 21, 2020. https://www2.deloitte.com/us/en/insights/industry/health-care/outpatient-virtual-health-care-trends.html.
7. Arnetz, Judith E. 2022, February. "The Joint Commission's New and Revised Workplace Violence Prevention Standards for Hospitals: A Major Step Forward Toward Improved Quality and Safety." *Joint Commission Journal on Quality and Patient Safety* 48 (4): 241–5. https://doi.org/10.1016/j.jcjq.2022.02.001

Glossary of Terms

Ambulatory and Alternate Care Sites (AACS) Buildings or suites where health care services are offered by health care professionals in outpatient settings, away from the hospital. Examples include physician offices, health clinics, immediate cares, physical rehabilitation centers, ambulatory surgery centers, dental offices, hospital outpatient departments, diagnostic imaging centers, home health, hospice, dialysis centers, residential care, skilled nursing facilities, rehabilitation centers, nursing homes, and assisted living facilities.

Canadian Centre for Occupational Health and Safety (CCOHS) An independent departmental corporation under the Financial Administration Act that is accountable to Parliament through the Ministry of Labour that functions as the primary national agency in Canada for the advancement of safe and healthy workplaces by preventing work-related injuries, illnesses, and deaths, by providing information, training, education, and management systems and solutions.

Internal Response Team (IRT) A team within an organization trained to respond to active situations of violence or escalation to remediate individuals in behavioral crisis. Also often called: Behavioral Escalation Support Team (BEST) or Behavioral Emergency Response Team (BERT) or "Code Gray" or "Code White."

International Association of Health Care Security and Safety (IAHSS) A professional association dedicated to professionals involved in managing and directing security and safety programs in health care facilities. IAHSS has more than 2,000 members who are health care security, law enforcement, safety, and emergency management leaders who work to establish best practices and guidelines for the industry.

Occupational Safety and Health (OSH) Committee A team of people within an organization that identifies and mitigates safety hazards and risks in the workplace to prevent and minimize injury and illness on the job. This team will facilitate training on safety standards, review current safety issues, conduct accident investigations, and perform hazard assessments to identify health and safety issues/gaps and develop strategies and recommendations to make the work environment safe.

Occupational Safety and Health Administration (OSHA) A large regulatory agency of the U.S. Federal Department of Labor that ensures safe and healthful working conditions for workers by setting and enforcing standards and by providing training, outreach, education, and assistance.

Providers An individual health care professional licensed to provide diagnosis and treatment services including medication, surgery, and medical devices. Examples of providers include Nurse Practitioners, Nurse Midwives, Nurse Anesthetists, Physician Assistants, and Physicians.

Rounding Walking through workplace departments to perform regular, informal check-ins with employees (similar to medical staff making patient rounds). It can be used to assess morale, demonstrate engagement, confirm compliance, etc.

Threat Assessment Team (TAT) A team or committee that convenes to assess a WPV incident or threat to coordinate an organizational response in a unified and efficient way. (For example, if a patient threatens a nurse, the team will decide if the threat is significant and how best to counter it. They will gather facts like the patient's medical and mental diagnoses, current stressors, ability to cause harm, weapon ownership, circumstances that triggered the threat, and whether they have previous incidents, to decide an appropriate response.)

Workplace Violence (WPV) Any act or threat of physical violence, harassment, intimidation, or other threatening disruptive behavior that occurs at the work site.

Workplace Violence Prevention (WPVP) A system of attitudes, strategies, practices, initiatives, and behaviors that work to stop and prevent any acts of threat, harassment, intimidation, or disruptive behavior from occurring at a place of employment.

CHAPTER 10
Best Practices and Additional Resources

Kimberly A. Urbanek and Kyle J. Graham

When applying **workplace violence prevention (WPVP)** strategies to real life, there are many learning points that surface. On occasion, there are also unintended consequences or pitfalls to watch out for when implementing new initiatives. **Workplace violence (WPV)** regulations that were once suggestions have now evolved into mandatory requirements for organizations. These requirements provide guidance to organizations on what is needed, but often lack the steps to explain "how to" when developing solutions. Therefore, this chapter provides additional references and resources to help iron out how to apply concepts. It can be used to advance and standardize an organization's WPVP program and can provide additional information and research to draw from. This chapter is meant to serve as a repository of ideas and best practices gathered from leading experts in the field.

Going forward, this handbook will evolve to include new research and best practice strategies as new ideas surface, so that prevention efforts can remain practical and relevant. Individuals and organizations are encouraged to send in their own ideas, successes, pain points, and initiatives for consideration in future versions. Readers are encouraged to provide honest feedback and input so that the health care industry can continue to learn, adapt, and grow in the quest to manage and eliminate WPV from the health care industry.

Please submit all feedback, requests, ideas, and best practices via e-mail to the authors at:

WPVPHandbook@gmail.com

Disclaimer

The ideas and best practices discussed here are compilations and examples from individual experiences reflecting real-life practices. Every effort has been made to ensure the information is accurate. The effectiveness and results may vary when implementing these practices depending on the needs and makeup of an organization, as well as how strategies are adopted. There is no guarantee of a particular outcome when utilizing a particular strategy or resource. Each organization needs to analyze and evaluate whether or not ideas listed here are appropriate for their facility. In addition, if utilizing one of the presented resources, an organization is bound to that resource's copyright rules. There is no intent to infringe on other's material and information is shared under the Fair Use Law for educational purposes only. The authors and contributors specifically disclaim any and all liability for any claims or damages that may result from providing this handbook and the information it contains.

Chapter 1: Workplace Violence in the Health Care Industry—An Introduction

There are many ways that an organization can participate in research or can utilize current surveys to evaluate how WPV incidents fluctuate annually. Below are some organizations that perform annual surveys specific to health care and are leaders in research and education.

- The **International Association of Health Care Security and Safety (IAHSS)** is one of those organizations and has established a foundation that does all of this work (IAHSSF)—IAHSSF. org. Recent research surveys and publications include crime statistics in health care, security challenges around COVID-19, Preventing Patient Abuse, and Preventing Patient Self-Harm. Participation in research and surveys helps advance the data needed to mitigate and prevent violence in health care. Crime surveys are also conducted annually (Figure 10.1).

- American Hospital Association—Case Studies
https://www.aha.org/2021-12-03-workforce-and-workplace-violence-prevention-case-studies

> **From the IAHSSF Website**
>
> IAHSSF, the International Association for Health Care Security and Safety Foundation, was founded in 1981 as the philanthropic arm of IAHSS. The International Association for Health Care Security and Safety Foundation was established to foster and promote the welfare of the public through educational and scientific research and development of health care security and safety body of knowledge.
>
> IAHSSF promotes and develops educational research into the maintenance and improvement of health care security and safety management as well as develops and conducts educational programs for the public.

Figure 10.1: IAHSSF Website: IAHSSF.org

Chapter 2: Building a Workplace Violence Prevention Program

There are several reliable resources to utilize when establishing the basic foundations of a WPVP program. These resources offer examples of what to include in WPV policies, requirements to meet regulatory standards, and information on creating a WPV committee.

Program Basics

- **U.S. Occupational Safety and Health Administration (OSHA)**
  https://www.osha.gov/workplace-violence
- **Canadian Centre for Occupational Health and Safety Regulations (CCOHS)** (Figure 10.2)
  http://laws-lois.justice.gc.ca/eng/regulations/sOR-86-304/index.html

> **Important Information about Canadian Occupational Health and Safety Regulations**
>
> All of the Canadian provinces have their own Occupational Health and Safety Act/Legislation. Provincial legislation varies slightly between the provinces; however, the basics are very much the same. The respective legislation outlines the responsibilities of the following:
>
> Government (provincial/federal) Responsibilities
> Employee (includes contracted staff/learners) Rights and Responsibilities
> Employers'/Supervisors' Responsibilities
> Requirements/Roles/Responsibilities for a Joint (Employer/Employee) Occupational Health & Safety Committee
>
> Under each of the Provincial Occupational Health and Safety Acts there are sections that speak to hazard identification/prevention (this includes but is not limited to WPV), education/training (to prevent/protect the workers from the hazard), and effective means of monitoring the hazards (measurement).

Figure 10.2: Canadian Centre for Occupational Health and Safety Regulations

Policies/Guidelines

- The **Joint Commission**—jointcommission.org
  For information on WPV regulations:
  s://www.jointcommission.org/search/#q=workplace%20
  violence&t=_Tab_All&sort=relevancy&f:_SitesOrganizations=
  [The%20Joint%20Commission]

- IAHSS Policy Guidelines
  https://www.iahss.org/page/hcsindustryguidelines

- U.S. Department of Labor
  https://www.dol.gov/agencies/oasam/centers-offices/human
  -resources-center/policies/workplace-violence-program

- American Hospital Association Guide to Creating Safer
  Workplaces   https://www.aha.org/guidesreports/2021-10-26
  -creating-safer-workplaces-guide-mitigating-violence-health
  -care-settings

Policy Example

Organizations should work to establish comprehensive policies for
WPV. Figure 10.3 provides a sample of a WPV policy that can be used
as a starting point. This sample offers a foundation that can be built
upon to create a customized policy detailing specifics to an organization.

WPV Committees

Some of the personnel to consider for inclusion on the WPV committee
include:

- Upper-Level Management (with Decision-Making authority)
- Public Safety/Security Leadership
- Risk Management Personnel
- **Occupational Safety and Health** Personnel
- Human Resources Manager
- Clinical Leadership from high-risk areas (Emergency Depart-
  ment, Critical Care, etc.)
- Behavioral Health Leadership
- Ambulatory and Alternate Care Sites Leader

[Company Name] Health Care—WPV Policy

WPV is any act or threat of physical violence, harassment, intimidation, or other threatening disruptive behavior that occurs at the work site. It ranges from threats and verbal abuse to physical assaults and even homicide. This may include, but is not limited to:

- intentional physical injury to another person,
- verbal or written threats of violence/intimidation,
- any physical behavior that involves aggressive physical contact with any other person including pushing, hitting, fighting, striking, and throwing objects,
- aggressive or hostile behavior that creates a reasonable fear of injury to another person,
- any act of vandalism or intentional damage to employer/employee property,
- possession of prohibited weapons, including firearms, knives, sprays, shock device, other item or device that could harm/injure, or any form of weapon or explosive restricted under local, state, or federal regulation,
- retaliatory actions against an individual who reported a WPV incident as required by this policy.

[Company Name] is committed to providing a safe work environment and does not tolerate any type of WPV committed by or against employees. [Company Name] strives to eliminate violence and promote the health and well-being of employees, physicians, volunteers, patients, and visitors and mitigate and prevent acts of violence. This commitment is jeopardized when any person, including [Company Name] employees, commits any act of violence in the workplace, or when any [Company Name] employee is the victim of violence in the workplace. This plan has been developed to provide procedures that will address the identification, prevention, response, and management of violent acts or threats of violence, with the overall goal to enhance safety for all. Violations of this policy may result in discipline up to and including immediate discharge. Employees should also understand that such behavior may also be criminal and could result in criminal prosecution.

Recognition/Identification: Every employee shares responsibility for maintaining a safe work environment. Employees are expected to participate in timely reporting of potentially escalating or dangerous situations. WPV incidents must be immediately reported to [Supervisor/Security/Law Enforcement, etc.]

Prevention: WPV Awareness Training is provided to all [Company Name] employees annually, to help them recognize potential acts of WPV, which will provide the opportunity to prevent these incidents before they occur. All staff will also be trained on how to report WPV incidents. Additional prevention training will be provided to employees in high-risk areas to develop their skills in de-escalation and response to acts of violence. All employees are trained on how to activate response teams to call for assistance for actively violent situations.

Response/Threat Management: (List appropriate internal response plan and how ongoing threats are managed [**Threat Assessment Team**, etc.])

Postvention: [Company Name] has resources available to assist staff when they are involved in, or witness, a violent or highly stressful incident. These resources include [List out available resources.]

Figure 10.3: WPV Policy Template

- Patient/Family Advisor or Patient Advocate
- Physician/Medical Director
- Legal Advisors
- Marketing/Public Relations personnel
- Union Leadership (if necessary, based on contract)
- Insurance Management Personnel (Claims or Employee Health)

Canadian Health and Safety Regulations also provide resources for how to establish a WPV Committee for Canadian Health Care Organizations.

- Canadian Occupational Health and Safety Regulations
  http://laws-lois.justice.gc.ca/eng/regulations/sOR-86-304/index
  .html

Health care facilities across Canada should have functioning Joint Occupational Health and Safety Committees (JHSC) (these are legislated and vary in size based on the number of employees). The JHSC by definition is a joint collaborative committee between the employer and employee with the purpose of improving worker safety. WPV and WPVP must be a standing agenda item at JHSC meetings. In some cases, the JHSC may serve as the WPVP committee. In others where the risk/incident rate of WPV is greater, the organization should have a separate WPVP committee. The WPVP committee should include representatives from across the organization (employee and employer reps.) including members of the executive leadership team. The WPVP committee should have unrestricted access to data/metrics/watch indicators, access/authority to complete risk assessment/identification, and be empowered to help identify areas for improvement (education/training).

Chapter 3: Workplace Violence Internal Response and Follow-Up

Internal Response Teams

When creating **Internal Response Teams (IRTs)** determine what is needed and what team(s) to create to respond to active incidents.

1. Choose a name for the type of response needed.
   - Behavioral Emergency Response Team (B.E.R.T.)
   - Behavioral Escalation Support Team (B.E.S.T.)

- Ambulatory Emergency Response Team (A.R.T.)
- Code Gray/Code White/Dr. Strong

2. Determine who needs to be on the team.
3. Determine how to activate the team.
4. Create roles and responsibilities for the team (Figure 10.4).

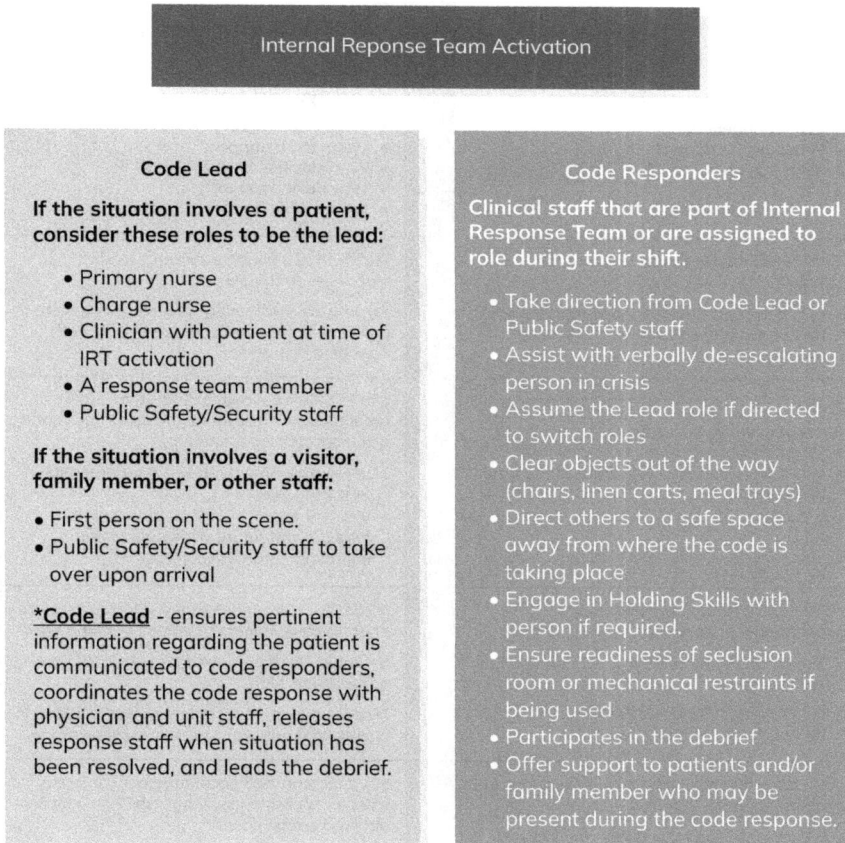

Internal Reponse Team Activation

Code Lead

If the situation involves a patient, consider these roles to be the lead:

- Primary nurse
- Charge nurse
- Clinician with patient at time of IRT activation
- A response team member
- Public Safety/Security staff

If the situation involves a visitor, family member, or other staff:

- First person on the scene.
- Public Safety/Security staff to take over upon arrival

*Code Lead - ensures pertinent information regarding the patient is communicated to code responders, coordinates the code response with physician and unit staff, releases response staff when situation has been resolved, and leads the debrief.

Code Responders

Clinical staff that are part of Internal Response Team or are assigned to role during their shift.

- Take direction from Code Lead or Public Safety staff
- Assist with verbally de-escalating person in crisis
- Assume the Lead role if directed to switch roles
- Clear objects out of the way (chairs, linen carts, meal trays)
- Direct others to a safe space away from where the code is taking place
- Engage in Holding Skills with person if required.
- Ensure readiness of seclusion room or mechanical restraints if being used
- Participates in the debrief
- Offer support to patients and/or family member who may be present during the code response.

Figure 10.4: IRT Activation

Postvention/Debriefing Options

The Crisis Prevention Institute (CPI) utilizes the Coping Model for post incident debriefing. This model (Figure 10.5) is used twice, once when debriefing with the offender and once when debriefing with the staff who intervened. There is value in completing both debriefings.

The *COPING Model* SM

INDIVIDUAL		STAFF
CONTROL – Ensure that emotional and physical control is regained. • I'd like to talk about what happened earlier. Do you have a few minutes?	**C**	**CONTROL** – Ensure that emotional and physical control is regained by the staff. Start the conversation by acknowledging staff's feelings and then asking permission to discuss.
ORIENT yourself to the basic facts. • What happened? • When did it happen? • Who else has been affected? • Why did it happen? • Where did it happen?	**O**	**ORIENT** yourself to the basic facts. • What happened? • When did it happen? • Who else has been affected? • Why did it happen? • Where did it happen?
PATTERNS – Look for patterns for the behavior. • Is this the first time the individual reacted that way, or has it become a recurring event?	**P**	**PATTERNS** – Look for patterns in staff responses to the behavior. Review the staff response history. Are there patterns in how the team or specific staff members responded?
INVESTIGATE alternatives to the behavior. • What could you do differently next time? • What should we do to put things right? • What were you thinking about at the time of the incident?	**I**	**INVESTIGATE** ways to strengthen staff responses. With team members, propose and discuss potential solutions. • What were you thinking about at the time of the incident? • What changes should be considered to help prevent future crisis events or to improve a future response?
NEGOTIATE future approaches and expectations of behavior. • What can we do to help you when you feel distressed? • Is there anything you don't want us to do during these moments?	**N**	**NEGOTIATE** changes that will improve future interventions. Reinforce what's working well. Example: "Is there anything you would have done differently?" Discuss and gain commitment from all staff to ensure that any improvements will be made.
GIVE back responsibility; provide support and encouragement. • I appreciate you talking with me. Do you agree with the plan that we just discussed?	**G**	**GIVE** support and encouragement. Express trust and confidence in their ability to respond during the next crisis.

Figure 10.5: The CPI COPING Model

Figure 10.6 is another example of a post incident debriefing document that could be used following a WPV incident. It should be noted that this tool is meant to specifically evaluate the staff response. No patient data is documented on the form, although it could be, as

INCIDENT DEBRIEFING DOCUMENT

**** TO BE COMPLETED BY STAFF INVOLVED IN INCIDENT****

Type of Incident: ☐ Verbal ☐ Physical ☐ Code Activation ☐ IRT ☐ Restraint ☐ Workplace Violence Incident ☐ Other

Offender Involved: ☐ Patient ☐ Visitor ☐ Family Member ☐ Student ☐ Other:

Name of Person Leading Debrief:	**Date of Incident:**	**Time of Incident:**

Other Staff Involved:

Building:	**Department:**	**Specific Location:**

Any Verbal Abuse:	No	Yes	**Any Injuries:** No	Yes (Describe)
Any Physical Abuse:	No	Yes (Describe)		

Brief Description of Event: (Examples of Behaviors witnessed)

What behavior level(s) were displayed: (Check all that apply)
☐ **Anxiety** – An increase in energy; change in typical behavior.
☐ **Defensive** – Verbal acting out; Protecting oneself from a real or perceived harm or challenge.
☐ **Risk Behaviors** – Physical acting out; behavior that presents an imminent or immediate risk to self or others.
☐ **Tension Reduction** – After the crisis; Decrease in physical and emotional energy and output.

Attempted Staff Approaches/Interventions: (Check all that apply)

Supportive Approach	☐ Active Listening ☐ Acknowledgement ☐ Comfort Measures ☐ Allow space / time ☐ Validates Experience
Directive Approach /De-escalation	☐ Decreased Stimuli ☐ Verbal Support ☐ Buddy System ☐ Used Compassionate Curiosity ☐ Common Goal Building ☐ Limit Setting ☐ Offered Choices and Consequences ☐ Distraction techniques ☐ Relate to person /use empathy ☐ Activated IRT/Code ☐ Ignored Challenges ☐ Redirected ☐ Listened /Allowed Venting ☐ Other:
Safety Interventions	☐ Activated Code Response ☐ Called Security ☐ Removed Subject ☐ Cleared Room /Hazards ☐ Medicated ☐ Called 911 ☐ Restrained ☐ Initiated 1:1 ☐ Monitoring ☐ Quiet Room ☐ Other:
Therapeutic Rapport	☐ Rebuilt Trust ☐ Debriefed with Subject ☐ Negotiated Next Steps ☐ Established Expectations ☐ Behavior Agreement
No Intervention Techniques	☐ Due to Imminent Safety Risk ☐ No opportunity /Quick escalation
Outcomes:	☐ Verbally De-escalated ☐ De-escalated after intervention ☐ Removed from Property ☐ Left on their own ☐ Team De-escalation ☐ Terminated from Care ☐ Trespassed ☐ Arrested ☐ Completed Report ☐ Other:

What went well / should be reinforced?

What opportunities are there for improvement?

Reminder* Resources available for Staff Mental Health include: (add resources here)
*Give completed form to Supervisor

Figure 10.6: Incident Debriefing Document

determined by the individual organization. This form guides the debriefing conversation and clearly shows if staff response was in alignment with offender behaviors. It also helps re-educate on other de-escalation techniques that could have been attempted.

Chapter 4: Gathering Data: It Must Be Measured to Be Managed

Data Collection

There are a lot of data points that can be collected to help identify specifics about violence, training deficits, high risk areas, etc. Some key data points to collect are noted in Table 10.1.

Depending on what information you are looking to track, there are some additional data points to consider in addition to those in Table 10.1, in order to obtain the desired information. These include:

- *Incident Location*—helps determine high-risk areas and frequency. Be as specific as possible.
- *Incident Severity* (including Lost Time Medical Aid—LTMA)—also determines high-risk areas and what level of training is needed.
- *Location Day/Time*—By tracking the day of the week and the time of the day, you can determine which days of the week and which hours have the highest frequency. This can also be cross-referenced by department. So, if the mental health unit has the most injuries on Tuesdays between 5 pm and 8 pm, this data can help drive decisions around adequate staffing on shift, adequate resources, supervisor presence at that time of day, etc.
- *Staff Training Data*—Track the training level of the staff that were injured to determine their skill level. Staff training might only be at the awareness level, or training in verbal de-escalation, or verbal/physical, or advanced intervention skills, etc. This can help drive training needs or remediation needs in specific areas.
- *Staff Resources on Shift* at time of occurrence—May drive staffing ratios.

Table 10.1: Important WPV Data Points to Collect

Date of Incident
Time of Incident
Building/Location of Incident
Department/Unit Where Incident Occurred
Offender Name
Offender Type (Patient/Visitor/Student/Staff/Provider/etc.)
Offender Gender
Offender Age
Summary of Event
Victim(s) Name
Victim(s) Type (Patient/Visitor/Student/Staff/Provider/etc.)
Victim Job Title (Nurse/Technician/Public/Safety/Mental Health/Registration/Other, etc.)
Verbal Event (Yes/No)
Type of Verbal Event: • Anxiety • Challenging/Untrusting • Refusal/Uncooperative • Yelling/Screaming • Threatening
Physical Contact (Yes/No)
Any injuries? (Yes/No)
Injury Data (Location of Injury, Mechanism of Injury)
Is it a reportable incident? (OSHA Reportable/Sentinel Event?)
Any lost work days/modified duty?

Documenting Data

Once collected, data should be captured in a spreadsheet or somewhere that would yield a fuller picture of the incidents. Data can also be graphed if desired. Tracking each piece of data allows flexibility to dial down and identify problem areas.

Figure 10.7 demonstrates how to collect important data points from several incidents in a spreadsheet format. Figure 10.8 is a continuation of the spreadsheet in Figure 10.7 and demonstrates how individual actions can be captured in the appropriate categories. Some of these categories

INCIDENT #	DATE	TIME	ID	DEPARTMENT/ LOCATION	SUMMARY	SEX	AGE	STATUS
22-0037213	5/1/2022	1.31 AM	Hosp	EMERGENCY DEPT	Intoxicated t. was flailing, punching the bed, & taunting PSOs.	M	43	Patient
22-0037228	5/1/2022	10:00 PM	Clinic	PAIN CLINIC	Pt. became verbally abusive & attempted to hit an RN during a procedure.	M	43	Patient
22-0037237	5/2/2022	8:23 PM	Hosp	CRITICAL CARE	As RN was speaking to a pt, the pt. proceeded to kick her in the abdomen.	M	10	Patient
22-0037276	5/4/2022	9.21 AM	Hosp	EMERGENCY DEPT	Pt. who left AMA was verbally aggressive, & making threats of physical harm. After being escorted out, pt attempted to spit on Officers, & made threats. Police responded.	M	55	Patient
22-0037280	5/4/2022	11:01 AM	Hosp	EMERGENCY DEPT	Pt. in police custody was spitting, kicking, calling staff vulgarities & racial slurs, & threatened to kill everyone.	M	55	Patient
22-0037282	5/4/2022	12:10 PM	Hosp	EMERGENCY DEPT	Father of pt. became upset & refused to leave when informed of the updated visitor policy. He then engaged in a verbal altercation w/staff. While being escorted out by Public Safety, the subject told Officers they should fear for their life.	M	-	Visitor

Figure 10.7: Example of Data Spreadsheet to Calculate WPV Stats (Part 1)
Adapted from Fleming, Bradley A. n.d. "Workplace Violence Data Spreadsheet."

BITE (A)	BITE	BLT OBJ	BDY FL	COM	GRB	HIT (A)	HIT	SCR (A)	SCR	SXL ASLT	THR	VRB	RACE RLTD	CONTACT NO INJURY	CONTACT W/INJURY	LOCATION OF INJURY	TITLE
				X								X					
						X						X					
							X								Y	Torso	RN
			X								X	X	X				
			X			X						X					
												X					

Figure 10.8: Example of Data Spreadsheet to Calculate WPV Stats (Part 2)
Adapted from Fleming, Bradley A. n.d. "Workplace Violence Data Spreadsheet."

include bite, attempted bite, object thrown, bodily fluids (spit), grab, attempted hit, hit, attempted scratch, scratch, sexual assault, threats, verbal aggression, race related, contact but no injury, contact with injury, location of injury, title of victim, etc. There are several other categories that could be included, but these are just a few. These individual stats allow an organization to really hone in on the specifics of violence so that they can focus prevention efforts toward the most egregious areas.

Chapter 5: Executive Ownership: Leading from the Front

There are many resources available regarding leadership responsibilities in WPVP. These responsibilities include how leadership can visibly support prevention efforts, how they can supply staff with the necessary tools and training, and how they create a **culture** of prevention. Additional resources around culture management are listed in Chapter 7.

- The CEO Coalition, a newly formed organization for CEOs of Health Care organizations where they can declare their commitment to enhancing staff safety. This is one way for leadership within the industry to ensure that staff feel heard and are aware of leadership support. https://www.ceocoalition.com/

From the CEO Coalition Website

CEO COALITION   Newsroom   Join Us

In early 2021, CEOs from leading hospitals and health systems across the U.S. convened virtually to examine standards of safety and trust for healthcare team members at every level of their organizations. Their goal was to collectively take action to protect the well-being of these essential team members and ensure that they have the systems, tools, technologies, and resources they need and deserve to feel safe at work. These discussions resulted in a Declaration of Principles for the physical and emotional safety and just treatment of all who work in healthcare. Their work kicks off a national movement and action plan to turn these Principles into meaningful change.
We invite healthcare CEOs across the country to catalyze the work by joining the Coalition Founders to renew and expand the definition of safety for a better, more inclusive future of caring.

- My American Nurse notes how executive support is needed and shares necessary leadership responsibilities in regard to WPV. https://www.myamericannurse.com/wp-content/uploads/2020/09/an9-Workplace-violence.pdf

Violence Risk Assessment Tools

Leaders need to provide the sufficient tools, training, and resources for staff to remain safe. Violence Risk Assessment tools provide a standard way to assess behaviors for potential violence. An assessment is completed, and based on the score, a level of risk will be determined. This can serve as a proactive communication to alert staff of necessary precautions. Some tools to consider implementing to proactively assess for violence include:

- Violence Aggression and Assessment Checklist (VAAC) (Figure 10.9): https://www.oahhs.org/assets/documents/files/5a%20WPV %20risk%20assessment%20tool.pdf (Section 5A)

Assessment Tool:

TYPE OF BEHAVIOUR EXHIBITED	YES/NO	DESCRIPTORS
History of Violence	☐ Yes ☐ No	History of being physically aggressive towards a caregiver.
Uncooperative	☐ Yes ☐ No	Easily annoyed or angered. Unable to tolerate the presence of others. Will not follow instructions.
Verbal Abuse	☐ Yes ☐ No	Verbal attacks, abuse, name calling, verbally neutral comments uttered in a snarling, aggressive manner.
Hostile/Attacking Objects	☐ Yes ☐ No	Overtly loud or noisy, i.e., slams doors, shouts out when talking, etc. An attack directed at an object and NOT at an individual, i.e., the indiscriminate throwing of an object, banging or smashing windows, kicking, banging, head-banging, smashing of furniture
Threats	☐ Yes ☐ No	A verbal outburst which is more than just a raised voice; and where there is definite intent to intimidate or threaten another person. A definite intent to physically threaten another person, i.e., raising of arm/leg, aggressive stance, making a fist, etc.
Assaultive/Combative	☐ Yes ☐ No	An application of force or attack directed at an individual, i.e., kick, punch, spit, grabbing of closthing, use of a weapon or weapon of opportunity.

Figure 10.9: Example of VAAC Tool
Adapted from the Broset Violence Checklist (R. Almvik, & P. Woods, 2000); Alert System Risk Indicator (R. King et al., 2006); and Correlates of Accuracy in the Assessment of Psychiatric Inpatients' Risk of Violence (D. McNeil, & R. Binder, 1995) Developed by PSHSA 2010. All rights reserved.

Scoring Tool:

Behavior	Level of Risk	Intervention
No Observed Behavior	LOW	No intervention required
History or Uncooperative or Verbal abuse	MODERATE (Intervention required)	List Intervention or refer to policies and procedures
Any One (1) or more in shaded area or TWO (2) or more in Non-Shaded area	HIGH (Preventative Measures Required)	List Measures or refer to policies and procedures

Figure 10.9: Example of VAAC Tool (*Continued*)

- Broset Violence Checklist (BVC)
  https://www.frenzs.org/bvc-broset-violence-checklist/?campai
  gnid=16617326042&adgroupid=135092834856&network=g&
  gclid=EAIaIQobChMIvaT-wZnL9wIV5x6tBh3LYwJ1EAAYASA
  AEgLxZfD_BwE

- Centers for Diseases Control and Prevention and The National
  Institute for Occupational Safety and Health (NIOSH)
  https://wwwn.cdc.gov/WPVHC/Nurses/Course/Slide/Unit6_8

Chapter 6: Managing Training and Education Needs

De-escalation Drills

Conducting de-escalation drills in high-risk areas is very beneficial to staff. A drill can consist of role-play where one person will serve as the patient and will act out a common example of escalation based on a predetermined scenario, while other staff serve as the caregivers and responders to the incident. This allows staff to practice critical thinking and apply de-escalation concepts in real time in a safe environment. Drills can also be conducted off of the unit in a classroom or simulation lab. Each drill should be debriefed as most of the key learning points will be highlighted as to what the strengths and opportunities were with each interaction. As drills are repeated, staff will get more comfortable and will create "muscle memory" in how to respond appropriately and successfully.

Scripting Ideas

Training can be enhanced by creating actual scripting for staff or "conversation starters" to help staff apply concepts in a practical way. It is common for staff to "not know what to say" or for staff to immediately try to share and enforce policies, set limits, or give ultimatums. There are many techniques that can be employed prior to responding in a stern way. Focus on the four areas in Figure 10.10 when providing de-escalation training to staff. Work on specific ways to enhance

1. Acknowledging to validate feelings
   Staff often don't know how to properly acknowledge an upset person. Instead, they often debate the veracity of what was just said. It's important for staff to first hear what was said, prior to trying to change the person's opinion.

   Examples:
   - I'm sorry it's been so tough for you.
   - That must be really scary/frustrating/difficult/etc.
   - I can understand why you'd be upset. I'd probably feel the same way.

2. Approach with compassionate curiosity
   Staff should be inquisitive before they correct someone. They should seek to gain a better understanding of what is being communicated by the acting out behaviors.

   Examples:
   - Can you please tell me more about that?
   - What would help you right now?
   - Has something changed to make you feel this way?

3. Set common goals
   Staff should use a mentality of partnership. Staff should expect cooperation and not compliance as that often creates resistance to being told what to do.

   Examples:
   - Can we work together to make this happen?
   - We are on the same team.
   - How can we work to resolve this?

4. Set Limits

   Examples:
   - It's not ok to use abusive language.
   - I'll be able to listen as soon as your voice is as calm as mine.
   - Your yelling is making others uncomfortable. Please lower your voice.

Figure 10.10: Examples of Scripting Cheat Sheets for Staff

training transfer. Providing scripting examples helps staff truly learn better ways to de-escalate and provide verbal support. Scripting examples demonstrate to staff how to translate training concepts into practical application.

Staff Triggers and Bias

In addition to de-escalation training, staff should receive training about how to identify their own personal triggers. These triggers or job stressors can result in staff unintentionally becoming the escalator. Help staff understand what triggers them while at work. Identifying these stressors can raise their awareness and improve their patience when interacting with patients.

It's also important to be aware that personal bias can unknowingly influence decision-making and can affect how staff interact with patients. Studies show that patients with behavioral health or addiction conditions are treated differently than those without, even by health care professionals. Some examples of bias are:

- Denying comfort measures that would otherwise be provided to a patient (food, water, blankets, etc.)
- Telling a patient they need to "just relax" and "calm down" during a panic attack
- Spending less clinical time with behavioral patients than with other patients
- Belief that a "psych" patient is "manipulating the system"
- Refusing to dispense a drug that is needed
- Believing patients with substance use disorders are dangerous and unpredictable

There are several biases that staff may unknowingly carry. Common biases can include bias against age, gender, race, religion, sexual orientation, diagnosis, or disability. It is necessary to teach staff to look for their own bias and encourage them to accept individual differences. It's hard for people to believe they have bias so give practical examples for reference. Have staff reflect on the following questions about themselves to help them identify areas for improvement. Support them with ways to eliminate or reduce their bias.

- Do I refer to specific patients using derogatory terms?
- Do I label patients or use stigmatizing language? ("He's a schizophrenic" vs. "He has schizophrenia.")
- Do I treat mental health patients differently than other patients?
- Are my beliefs about mental health disorders consistent with research?
- Am I annoyed rather than sympathetic when caring for psychiatric patients?
- Do I think that certain individuals are beyond hope or help?
- Do I minimize or disregard their treatment preferences over my own preferences?

Chapter 7: Building a Culture of Violence Prevention

Building a **culture** of violence prevention is something that occurs over time. McKinsey notes that 70% of change efforts fail due to employee resistance and lack of management support. There are several resources on how to be successful and implement changes that last. Some key strategies to be successful with long-term improvements include utilizing **change management**, building trust and resilience with staff, getting staff engaged, and celebrating successes.

Change Management

- Transformational Change: Changing Change Management—
  McKinsey & Company
  Boris Ewenstein, Wesley Smith, and Ashvin Sologar
  https://www.mckinsey.com/featured-insights/leadership/
  changing-change-management

- Leading Change: 8 Reasons why Change Efforts Fail
  Book by John P. Kotter
  Training Website
  https://www.mastery.com/products/coursecatalog/info?
  courseid=tquelcks_vod&gclid=EAIaIQobChMIiuqzhqPL
  9wIVYQp9Ch2a4gK4EAAYASAAEgL95vD_BwE.

- Wharton Executive Education—Five Steps for Managing Culture Change
  https://executiveeducation.wharton.upenn.edu/thought-leadership/wharton-at-work/2014/09/managing-culture-change/#:~:text=To%20manage%20culture%20change%2C%20the,using%20the%20action%20steps%20below.

Building Trust and Team Engagement

Culture is dependent on staff engagement and building trusting relationships. Organizations need to involve every employee in the process of WPVP. Engaging staff and making them part of the problem-solving and implementation teams will be a critical step to getting them to take ownership. Through continuous quality improvement and feedback, staff will see positive changes that will evolve into more momentum and engagement. Staff ownership is the true indicator that culture change is occurring. It is important to note that de-escalation is also based on trust, engagement, and balance of power. Organizations must work on building these principles with their teams so that staff feel empowered and informed on how to model those same principles with patients and their families. It is crucial to develop trust and engagement between the organization, the team members, and the patients, in order to create a sustainable culture change. Some resources on how to effectively build these relationships include:

- Book: The Speed of Trust: The One thing That Changes Everything
  Stephen M. Covey and Rebecca R. Merrill
  https://www.speedoftrust.com/

- Leadership in Times of Uncertainty
  https://rhrinternational.com/wp-content/uploads/2021/07/Leadership-in-Times-of-Uncertainty-1.pdf

- Servant Leadership—A Journey into the Nature of Legitimate Power and Greatness
  Robert K. Greenleaf (ISBN 0-8091-2527-7)

Recognition/Celebrations

Be sure to create ways to recognize and celebrate wins while working on violence prevention. Celebrate increases in reporting, successful de-escalation attempts, and number of staff that have completed training. Share stories that demonstrate how staff can be empowered to make a difference. Be sure to communicate improvements and stats regularly and be transparent on the journey of violence prevention.

Given that WPV is hugely underreported in health care, it is important that recognition programs reward desired safety behaviors and not just low numbers. Take care not to reward employees or departments for achieving the lowest injury rate as this can motivate employees not to report safety incidents related to WPV. Some ideas to recognize team achievements around WPVP include:

- Share safety stories to learn new approaches in department meetings.
- Recognize a staff member who helped build a sense of safety among other staff.
- Share successful "De-escalation in Action" stories at shift change.
- Celebrate the department that increased their reporting percentage the most.
- Celebrate the department that had the highest percentage of debriefings per incident.

Chapter 8: The Balancing Act between Patient Advocacy and Staff Support

There are times when it seems like leadership must choose between what a patient wants and what the staff want. This can pit these two individuals against each other, eroding the desired cooperation. When patients demand an exception to the rule, it's important to consider consequences for making allowances. It's important to individualize care plans, so exceptions have to be made, but be cautious they don't undermine the expectations. There must be room to make exceptions, but there must be consistency in how the established expectations are supported. Accommodations/exceptions are allowable but must still work toward the agreed-upon expectations. Making exceptions cannot be the norm and cannot be rewarding noncompliance.

Partnership Agreement

Utilizing a partnership agreement can be very effective in rebuilding trust between the organization and the individual, while still setting limits and guidelines about expected behaviors. These "contracts" include a conversation with the offender which allows them to be heard, as well as gets agreement from them on expected behaviors going forward (Figure 10.11).

Dear _____,

Any behavior that interferes with or presents a danger of interfering with patient care or other business at [Company Name], whether by phone or in person, is considered unacceptable. Unacceptable behaviors at [Company Name] include:

- Threats of violence or use of unlawful force against anyone
- Behavior that is abusive or verbally offensive
- Comments and statements, spoken or in writing, that are condescending, demeaning, rude, hostile, or threatening toward any staff or patients
- Any behavior that creates fear or apprehension for other patients, family members, staff, or visitors
- Threats, harassment, bullying, coercion, intimidation, cursing, aggressive body language/posturing, sexual overtones, aggressive gestures, aggressive language, racial slurs, or inappropriate physical contact

Concerns:

[Company Name]'s concern(s) include:

- Inappropriate language, swearing, and tone of voice used at the front desk on 5/1/21
- Aggressive, threatening language speaking to Dr. Smith on phone on 5/2/21
- *Customize as needed*

[Offender Name]'s concern(s) include:

- Rude front desk staff member who rolled her eyes
- Lack of communication from Provider
- *Customize as needed*

Expectations:

Expectations [Company Name] has for [Offender Name] include:

- Professional and courteous communication to all staff and providers over the phone, through e-mail and in person
- See details in Patient Rights and Responsibilities
- *Customize as needed*

Expectations [Offender Name] can anticipate from [Company Name] include:

- Professional and courteous communication from all physicians and staff, over the phone and in person.

Figure 10.11: Example of a Partnership Agreement

- See details in Patient Rights and Responsibilities
- *Customize as needed*

I have reviewed the above information and understand the expectations for behavior. I also understand I am able to continue using [Company Name] for my health care services as long as I meet these behavior expectations. I understand if I continue to demonstrate unacceptable behavior, my relationship with [Company Name] may be terminated. This termination would be effective as of thirty (30) days from the date of the notice and I would only be able to use [Company Name] to seek Emergency Room care for my own emergency medical issues. All other care would need to be provided elsewhere.

- _____ I have received a copy of The Patient Rights and Responsibilities
- _____ I have read, understand, and agree to the presented Partnership Agreement
- _____ I understand that failure to follow this Partnership may result in a dismissal from [Company Name].
- _____ I am choosing to not agree to this Partnership Agreement and understand that this may lead to my dismissal from [Company Name]. A dismissal will not prohibit me from seeking emergency care services through the [Company Name] Emergency Departments.

Signatures:

[Offender Name] _____ Date: _____

[Staff Name/Title] _____ Date: _____

Figure 10.11: Example of a Partnership Agreement (*Continued*)

Chapter 9: Ambulatory and Alternate Care Sites

Ambulatory and Alternate Care Sites (AACS) can benefit from collaboration with other similar locations. Smaller organizations might also have less data to pull from, so it would be beneficial for them to partner with other organizations so they can learn from one another's experiences. Initiating sharing in this way is new for most organizations but can prove beneficial. Since many sites might be smaller organizations, there is great value to partner with other sites on policy, procedure development, data trends, and quality improvement. In addition, collaboration with larger health care organizations or hospitals will provide strategies that can be adapted to the AACS. By starting with the basics, AACS can establish the infrastructure needed to add customized initiatives to their locations that positively reduce WPV (Figure 10.12).

7 Steps of WPV at Ambulatory and Alternate Care Sites

Figure 10.12: Steps to WPV Basics in the AACS

WPV Committee

Start by building a WPV committee specifically for the AACS. Consider adding committee representation from the departments listed in Table 10.2.

Table 10.2: Common Roles and Areas for a WPV Committee in the AACS

Roles to Consider:
Senior Leader of Ambulatory Services
Manager/Director of Quality or Compliance
Patient Experience Representative/Patient Advocate
Clinical Educators
Nursing Managers/Nursing Supervisors
Manager/Supervisor of Registration Services
Physician
Nurse
Medical Assistant/Patient Care Technician
Behavioral Health Clinician
Manager of Greeters/Concierge
Manager of Public Safety
Risk Management for Ambulatory sites
Additional Areas to Include as Needed:
Lab/Phlebotomy
Imaging Services (X-ray, CT, MRI, Mammography, etc.)
Neurology/Pain Clinics
Rehabilitation Services
Behavioral Health Outpatient Services

Table 10.2: Common Roles and Areas for a WPV Committee in the AACS (*Continued*)

Diabetes Services
Weight Loss Clinic
Outpatient Surgery Centers
Family Medicine (FM)/Internal Medicine (IM)
Obstetrics (OB)/Gynecology (GYN)
Pediatrics
Medical Subspecialties (Allergy, Endocrinology, Rheumatology, etc.)
Surgical Subspecialties (Ears/Nose/Throat (ENT), Gastroenterology, Ortho, etc.)

Strategies to Implement in AACS

There are multiple initiatives that can be created to form a tool kit for WPVP in the AACS. Some ideas for initiatives that can be implemented include:

- Create/review the WPV policy to be inclusive of AACS.
- Create scripting for difficult situations and place reminders around for staff.
- Create troubleshooting tip sheet for common situations that cause escalation.
- Create an IRT response to promote a team approach for support during de-escalation.
- Create an alert flag in the medical record to proactively communicate about potentially violent patients.
- Create a video showing a typical patient visit that demonstrates the right and wrong ways of how staff utilize de-escalation techniques.
- Create a code word to better communicate about potentially violent individuals in the office.
- Create a WPV hazard checklist to assess the organizational space for security measures (locked doors, panic buttons, safe spaces, cameras, etc.).
- Designate a specific area in the space to move an upset person to.

- Review schedules for the next day to screen patient lists for known risks/history of issues.
- Get staff trained on prevention techniques.
- Create or attend Active Threat Training.
- Preprogram emergency numbers on phones.
- Role-play possible scenarios to practice verbal and physical responses.
- Reposition furniture for safety and quick escape.
- Clear unnecessary items that could be used as weapons.
- Conduct debriefings as necessary to follow-up with staff and enhance future interactions.
- Partner with providers/physicians to create a cohesive approach to managing escalating behaviors.

Glossary of Terms

Ambulatory and Alternate Care Sites (AACS) Buildings or suites where health care services are offered by health care professionals in outpatient settings, away from the hospital. Examples include physician offices, health clinics, immediate cares, physical rehabilitation centers, ambulatory surgery centers, dental offices, hospital outpatient departments, diagnostic imaging centers, home health, hospice, dialysis centers, residential care, skilled nursing facilities, rehabilitation centers, nursing homes, and assisted living facilities.

Canadian Centre for Occupational Health and Safety (CCOHS) An independent departmental corporation under the Financial Administration Act that is accountable to Parliament through the Ministry of Labour that functions as the primary national agency in Canada for the advancement of safe and healthy workplaces by preventing work-related injuries, illnesses, and deaths, by providing information, training, education, management systems and solutions.

Change Management The practice and process of supporting and helping people change their behaviors, attitudes, and/or work processes to achieve a desired business objective or outcome, with the goal of ensuring that it is successful long term.

Culture A set of shared attitudes, values, goals, and practices that characterize an institution or organization.

Internal Response Team (IRT) A team within an organization trained to respond to active situations of violence or escalation to remediate individuals in behavioral crisis. Also often called: Behavioral Escalation Support Team (BEST team) or Behavioral Emergency Response Team (BERT) or "Code Gray" or "Code White."

International Association of Health Care Security and Safety (IAHSS) A professional association dedicated to professionals involved in managing and directing security and safety programs in Health care facilities. IAHSS has more than 2,000 members who are health care security, law enforcement, safety and emergency management leaders who work to establish best practices and guidelines for the industry.

Occupational Safety and Health Administration (OSHA) A large regulatory agency of the U.S. Federal Department of Labor that ensures safe and healthful working conditions for workers by setting and enforcing standards and by providing training, outreach, education, and assistance.

Occupational Safety and Health (OSH) Committee A team of people that identify and mitigate safety hazards and risks in the workplace to prevent and minimize injury and illness on the job. This team will facilitate training on safety standards, review current safety issues, conduct accident investigations, and perform hazard assessments to identify health and safety issues/gaps and develop strategies and recommendations to make the work environment safe.

The Joint Commission The oldest and largest U.S. standards-setting and accrediting body in health care; an independent, not-for-profit organization in the United States that administers voluntary accreditation programs for hospitals and other health care organizations. A majority of U.S. state governments recognize The Joint Commission accreditation as a condition of licensure in order to receive governmental insurance reimbursements. The Joint Commission drives quality improvement and patient safety in health care through accreditation, certification, regulatory standards, and measurement and performance improvement areas. Previously called Joint Commission on Accreditation of Health Care Organizations (JCAHO), The Joint Commission accredits approximately 88% of U.S. hospitals (4477 hospitals) and 22,000 total U.S. health care organizations and programs.

Threat Assessment Team A team or committee that convenes to assess a WPV incident or threat to coordinate an organizational response in a unified and efficient way. (For example, if a patient threatens a nurse, the team will decide if the threat is significant and how best to counter it. They will gather facts like the patient's medical and mental diagnoses, current stressors, ability to cause harm, weapon ownership, circumstances that triggered the threat, and whether they have previous incidents, to decide an appropriate response.)

Workplace Violence (WPV) Any act or threat of physical violence, harassment, intimidation, or other threatening disruptive behavior that occurs at the work site.

Workplace Violence Prevention (WPVP) A system of attitudes, strategies, practices, initiatives, and behaviors that work to stop and prevent any acts of threat, harassment, intimidation, or disruptive behavior from occurring at a place of employment.

Glossary

Ambulatory and Alternate Care Sites (AACS) Buildings or suites where health care services are offered by health care professionals in outpatient settings, away from the hospital. Examples include physician offices, health clinics, immediate cares, physical rehabilitation centers, ambulatory surgery centers, dental offices, hospital outpatient departments, diagnostic imaging centers, home health, hospice, dialysis centers, residential care, skilled nursing facilities, rehabilitation centers, nursing homes, and assisted living facilities. (pp. 161, 188)

Behavior Contract A written document outlining expectations for an individual's behavior and the likely consequences for failing to uphold those expectations. (p. 139)

Be on the Look Out (BOLO) An alert or broadcast, often issued by Public Safety, to alert others about a suspicious or wanted person or vehicle. A BOLO typically contains descriptive, identifying information and a phone number to call if the person or vehicle is observed. (p. 111)

Canadian Centre for Occupational Health and Safety (CCOHS) An independent departmental corporation under the Financial Administration Act that is accountable to Parliament through the Ministry of Labour that functions as the primary national agency in Canada for the advancement of safe and healthy workplaces by preventing work-related injuries, illnesses, and deaths, by providing information, training, education, and management systems and solutions. (pp. 88, 161, 188)

Canadian Federation of Nurses Unions (CFNU) The Canadian Federation of Nurses Unions (CFNU) represents nearly 200,000 nurses and nursing students across Canada and in a variety of health care settings (www.nursesunions.ca). (p. 11)

Categories of Violence Categories of Violence can refer to the way that data is captured. It can be captured as Type 1, 2, 3, or 4; or as verbal versus physical; or as a single or multiple incident event. (p. 11)

Change management The practice and process of supporting and helping people change their behaviors, attitudes, and/or work processes to achieve a desired business objective or outcome, with the goal of ensuring that it is successful long term. (pp. 123, 188)

Chief Executive Officer (CEO) The senior-most executive of the health care entity, be it a system or an independent hospital. (p. 89)

Communication The ability to convey facts, concepts, or reasoning clearly to others, and to receive and understand the messages sent by others. (p. 75)

Continuous Quality Improvement (CQI) A quality management process that looks at processes, procedures, and outcomes with the intent to enhance and better operations. (p. 75)

Critical Incident Stress Debriefing (CISD) A specific, seven-step process where a supportive, crisis-focused discussion is facilitated with a small, homogeneous group of people who encountered a powerful traumatic event. It aims at reduction of distress and a restoration of group cohesion and unit performance. (pp. 52, 139)

Culture A set of shared attitudes, values, goals, and practices that characterize an institution or organization. (pp. 124, 189)

Culture of Safety Signage Marketing materials used by an organization to communicate the organization's stance on violence being unacceptable in the workplace and encouraging an atmosphere of healthy boundaries, and safe and respectful interpersonal interactions. (p. 139)

Diagnostic Center A facility that utilizes specialized equipment or testing to determine the nature of a medical condition. Diagnostic centers can include radiology services, imaging services, nuclear medicine, and pathology and laboratory services. (p. 11)

Elope/Elopement To leave without others knowing or being aware. (p. 11)

Emotional Debriefing A discussion that takes place shortly after a situation of violence that allows those involved to process and share the emotional impact of the violence, while also identifying coping skills and strategies to promote resiliency and decrease the chances of long-standing traumatic responses. (p. 140)

Employee Assistance Program (EAP) A work-based intervention program designed to assist employees in connecting to resources to help resolve personal stressors. (p. 140)

Employee Peer Support Program A program that is established within an organization to support employees after an incident of WPV and/or trauma. It can effectively promote employee resiliency and effective coping strategies to advance the psychological health and safety of staff. This program is meant to be a nonjudgmental, safe, and supportive relationship between two people who have a lived experience in common. (p. 52)

First Aid (FA) An injury where treatment was administered by a qualified first aider or self-administered. The injury did not require medical treatment by a professional medical practitioner. (p. 75)

Formal Training A learning session that has specific, consistent curriculum that would result in a documented certification or completion. Formal training provides a structured approach and has the same specified objectives and goals for each student. (p. 111)

Foundation A nonprofit organization that supports the programs and services of a local hospital. They operate independently from the hospital and have their own focus and goals, with the primary goal of raising money for its affiliate hospital(s) and to increase community awareness. (p. 111)

Harden the Target A term meaning to strengthen the security of a building or area in order to increase protection and remove or reduce opportunities of crime and violence. Examples of target hardening techniques can include physical modifications, such as secure locks and motion lights, as well as procedural elements like visitor screenings and general access control. (p. 111)

Hazard An object or process which may cause an injury. The object can be chemical, physical, biological and the process can be psychosocial. (p. 75)

Informal Training A learning session that happens outside of a structured classroom environment, and although it can have intended objectives, it tends to have more unique learning outcomes for each student. (p. 111)

Injury (I) A person being hurt by physical, chemical, biological, or psychosocial agents. The harm can be medical or mental. (p. 75)

Internal Response Team (IRT) A team within an organization trained to respond to active situations of violence or escalation to remediate individuals in behavioral crisis. Also often called: Behavioral Escalation Support Team (BEST) or Behavioral Emergency Response Team (BERT) or "Code Gray" or "Code White." (pp. 31, 53, 161, 189)

International Association of Health Care Security and Safety (IAHSS) A professional association dedicated to professionals involved in managing and directing security and safety programs in health care facilities. IAHSS has more than 2,000 members who are health care security, law enforcement, safety, and emergency management leaders who work to establish best practices and guidelines for the industry. (pp. 161, 189)

Key Performance Indicators (KPIs) A quantifiable measurement of performance over time for a specific objective. KPIs provide targets for teams to shoot for, milestones to gauge progress, and insights that help people across the organization make better decisions. (p. 31)

Lost Time (LT) An injury serious enough to warrant a health care provider to restrict an employee from their regular job duties for a specified period of time. The injured cannot resume the next scheduled full-duty shift. The day of the injury is not considered Lost Time. (p. 75)

Management Safety Climate (MSC) Survey A survey tool that utilizes feedback from employees to inform a critical risk analysis of safety-related concerns across the organization. (p. 32)

Mechanical Restraints A device that is used to restrain the movement of the whole or part of a person's body. Restraints are commonly used when an individual is displaying behaviors that may cause harm to themselves or someone else. (p. 53)

Medical Aid (MA) An injury where the person requires medical treatment provided by a professional medical practitioner. Medical Aid includes first aid administered by a professional medical practitioner. (p. 75)

Medical Aid No Lost Time An injury where the victim requires medical attention/aid and is able to resume work, but with medical restrictions. May also be called Modified Duty or Light Duty. (p. 75)

Mirroring A nonverbal form of active listening in which the listener reflects the affect and body language of the speaker in order to convey a sense of empathy and understanding. (p. 140)

Near-Miss An event where a person was not injured but came close to being injured. (p. 75)

Nonverbal Communication The message conveyed in conversation through facial expressions, gestures, tone of voice, volume of voice, body language, physical proximity, eye contact, appearance, etc. (p. 140)

Occupational Safety and Health Administration (OSHA) A large regulatory agency of the U.S. Federal Department of Labor that ensures safe and healthful working conditions for workers by setting and enforcing standards and by providing training, outreach, education, and assistance. (pp. 11, 32, 89, 162, 189)

Occupational Safety and Health (OSH) Committee A team of people within an organization that identifies and mitigates safety hazards and risks in the workplace to prevent and minimize injury and illness on the job. This team will facilitate training on safety standards, review current safety issues, conduct accident investigations, and perform hazard assessments to identify health and safety issues/ gaps and develop strategies and recommendations to make the work environment safe. (pp. 32, 161, 189)

Paraverbal Communication The parts of verbal communication beyond the words being spoken, including volume, pace (speed), rhythm, tone, pitch that contributes to the message being conveyed. (p. 140)

Partnership Agreement A written document outlining expectations for an individual's behavior and the likely consequences for failing to uphold those expectations. (p. 140)

Patient Safety Comprehensive programs in which health care organizations methodically track and reduce harm to patients (e.g., hospital-acquired infections, medical treatment errors, etc.) by counting harmful incidents, performing cause analyses, and implementing continual improvements to reduce future incidents. (p. 89)

Postvention An organized immediate, short-term, and long-term response in the aftermath of a suicide to promote healing and mitigate the negative effects of exposure to discuss the actions and thought processes involved in a particular clinical situation, encourage reflection, and incorporate improvement into future performance. (p. 53)

Providers An individual health care professional licensed to provide diagnosis and treatment services including medication, surgery, and medical devices. Examples of providers include Nurse Practitioners, Nurse Midwives, Nurse Anesthetists, Physician Assistants, and Physicians. (p. 162)

Public Safety A department in a health care system that has a broad span of responsibilities, some of which include managing safety and security incidents, responding to emergency incidents, de-escalating verbal and physical disturbances, assisting with keeping patients safe, handling credentialing and identification of staff, and managing parking responsibilities. Sometimes referred to as the "Security" or "Protection" department. (pp. 53,89, 112)

Return on Investment (ROI) A performance measure used to evaluate the efficiency or profitability of a program. ROI measures the program value or benefits, relative to the investment costs. (pp. 32, 89, 112)

Rounding Walking through workplace departments to regularly check in with employees (similar to medical staff making patient rounds). It can be used to assess morale, demonstrate engagement, confirm compliance, etc. (pp. 89, 112, 162)

Seclusion Room A space with a locked entrance/exit that is used as a form of environmental restraint. This space is used to confine a patient when they may be at risk of harming others. (p. 53)

Silo A system, process, or department that operates in isolation from others. (p. 11)

Soft language The use of a gentle tone of voice that is understanding, compassionate, and supportive. (p. 140)

The Joint Commission The oldest and largest U.S. standards-setting and accrediting body in health care; an independent, not-for-profit organization in the United States that administers voluntary accreditation programs for hospitals and other health care organizations. A majority of U.S. state governments recognize The Joint Commission accreditation as a condition of licensure in order to receive governmental insurance reimbursements. The Joint Commission drives quality improvement and patient safety in health care through accreditation, certification, regulatory standards, and measurement and performance improvement areas. Previously called Joint Commission on Accreditation of Health care Organizations (JCAHO), The Joint Commission accredits approximately 88% of U.S. hospitals (4477 hospitals) and 22,000 total U.S. health care organizations and programs. (pp. 111, 189)

Threat Assessment Team (TAT) A team or committee that convenes to assess a WPV incident or threat to coordinate an organizational response in a unified and efficient way. (For example, if a patient threatens a nurse, the team will decide if the threat is significant and how best to counter it. They will gather facts like the patient's medical and mental diagnoses, current stressors, ability to cause harm, weapon ownership, circumstances that triggered the threat, and whether they have previous incidents, to decide an appropriate response.) (pp. 32, 53, 89, 162, 190)

Training Transfer Applying knowledge and skills acquired during training to a targeted job or role; practical application of gained knowledge to real-life work scenarios (p. 124)

VESSA Leave Victims' Economic Security and Safety Act (VESSA) allows employees who are victims of violence to take up to 12 weeks of unpaid leave for any 12-month period to seek medical help and legal assistance. (p. 140)

Violence Prevention Climate Scale (VPCS) A survey tool to assess individual staff perceptions of the extent to which organization management creates a climate that helps discourage employee exposure to physical violence and verbal aggression. (p. 32)

Vitamin K An essential vitamin needed by the human body that plays a key role in helping blood blot to prevent excessive bleeding. (p. 124)

Workplace Bullying A persistent pattern of mistreatment from others in the workplace that causes either physical or emotional harm. It can include such tactics as verbal, nonverbal, psychological, and physical abuse, as well as humiliation. (p. 112)

Workplace Harassment (Ontario Definition)
a.   Engaging in a course of vexatious comment or conduct against a worker in a workplace that is known or ought reasonably to be known to be unwelcome, or
b.   Workplace sexual harassment; (p. 75)

Workplace Sexual Harassment (Ontario Definition)
a.   Engaging in a course of vexatious comment or conduct against a worker in a workplace because of sex, sexual orientation, gender identity, or gender expression, where the course of comment or conduct is known or ought reasonably to be known to be unwelcome, or
b.   Making a sexual solicitation or advance where the person making the solicitation or advance is in a position to confer, grant, or deny a benefit or advancement to the worker and the person

knows or ought reasonably to know that the solicitation or advance is unwelcome; (p. 76)

Workplace Violence Prevention (WPVP) A system of attitudes, strategies, practices, initiatives, and behaviors that work to stop and prevent any acts of threat, harassment, intimidation, or disruptive behavior from occurring at a place of employment (pp. 12, 33, 54, 76, 90, 112, 124, 162, 190)

Workplace Violence (WPV) Any act or threat of physical violence, harassment, intimidation, or other threatening disruptive behavior that occurs at the work site. (pp. 11, 33, 54, 76, 90, 112, 124, 162, 190)

Workplace Violence (WPV) (Ontario Definition)

  a. The exercise of physical force by a person against a worker, in a workplace, that causes or could cause physical injury to the worker,

  b. An attempt to exercise physical force against a worker, in a workplace, that could cause physical injury to the worker,

  c. A statement or behavior that is reasonable for a worker to interpret as a threat to exercise physical force against the worker, in a workplace, that could cause physical injury to the worker. (p. 76)

www.ingramcontent.com/pod-product-compliance
Lightning Source LLC
Chambersburg PA
CBHW060221030426
42335CB00015B/1804